Wealth Mastery for Women

12 Laws to Create Wealth Starting Today

A Collaboration of

Paula Fellingham and The Four Dames

Patricia Barnett

Julie Jones Hamilton

Lynn Kitchen

Marilyn Macha

Published by Efluential Publishing a division of Efluential Marketing LLC

www.EfluentialPublishing.com

First Printing November 2015

Dedications

I dedicate this book to my amazing husband, Dr. Gilbert Fellingham. His love and never-wavering support has been "the wind beneath my wings" for over 40 years. I also extend my deep appreciation to my precious children and children-in-law: Heidi; Missy and Darin; Angela and Darrel; Joy and Steve; Elise and Les; Danny and Amanda; David and Jackie; and Ben. What profound JOY you give me every day!

- Paula Fellingham

It is with heartfelt appreciation for my beloved husband, Richard and our magnificent children, Ross and Amber. You inspire me daily! To my beautiful mother, family, friends, mentors and colleagues, your presence is my cherished gift. In celebration of Wealth Mastery for Women, I dedicate this book to you, the reader. Within this very moment, you have the power to change the rest of your life. Believe in the Power of YOU!

- Patricia Barnett

I dedicate this book to YOU, the reader and to my beloved family Jimmy, Claira, Rodney, Noelle, Khalid, Gunnar and my grandchildren. I am living the life I love by the grace of my mentors who supported me along the way - Donna, Dick, Jim, Kathy, Mary, Stephanie and Kelly.

- Julie Jones Hamilton

I dedicate this book to my husband, David Rothgaber, to my mother, Pollyann Castle, and all my mentors throughout the years. I celebrate each reader knowing you shall receive herein the answers for which you search!

- Lynn Kitchen

I dedicate this book to all the courageous and powerful women who came before me, including my brave, loving mother and maternal grandmother; to my beautiful family, John Hardesty, Justin and Amy Williams and to the two most powerful little boys that I have the honor to know and love, my precious grandsons Preston and Cole Williams, who call me TO BE every day.

- Marilyn J. Macha

We offer our sincere appreciation to Cliff Pelloni & Damon Darnall of Efluential Publishing and to Mary Ring for your dedication in the creation of *Wealth Mastery for Women.*

Preface

We believe in miracles. We believe in little ones, medium-size ones, and massive miracles that take your breath away.

The miracle of meeting each other and coming together to create Wealth Mastery was a beautiful little miracle. The work itself – the principles, concepts, insights and inspiration that has become *Wealth Mastery for Women* – is a mighty miracle.

You see, we realize that the *12 Laws of Wealth Mastery* will be used to help women worldwide understand that wealth creation is not difficult. It is very possible and within the reach of every woman, everywhere.

The 12 Laws are amazingly simple. They are tried and true. When you begin at the beginning, with LAW ONE, reading *and* applying the action steps, moving forward each day toward your goals, massive miracles can be manifested in your life!

We'd love to hear from you! As you read, take action and see results in your life, we invite you to share your experiences. Please email us at *results@WealthMasteryforWomen.com*. We look forward to celebrating your WINS.

Introduction

The Creation of *Wealth Mastery for Women*

We acknowledge you for your desire to create the financial abundance that will bless your life and the lives of your loved ones, and we wish you the very best!

As with most things that endure, the friendship of Paula Fellingham, the Founder of The Women's Information Network (WIN) and The Four Dames: Patricia Barnett, Julie Jones Hamilton, Lynn Kitchen and Marilyn Macha began like a small seed and grew through the years into a strong, priceless relationship.

Over the years, Paula Fellingham and the powerful team of The Four Dames have crossed paths to support raising the awareness and individual potential for women everywhere. It is our intention to offer women the knowledge and the support of knowing that anything is possible and how to become the generator of your own wealth and life.

Our friendship unfolded naturally and with ease when Paula invited The Four Dames into a dialogue to explore the possibility of collaborating to create this wealth of information – The 12 Laws. From that moment a unique and rich relationship developed, driven by the same core values and vision, "We Are Women Helping Women Live Our Best Lives."

In *Wealth Mastery for Women, 12 Laws of Creating Wealth Starting Today*, Paula Fellingham and The Four Dames bring a combined 175 years of experience in the personal development industry as highly-trained experts in human potential and results achievement.

It is our desire to inform you, to inspire you, and to believe in you as you read through *Wealth Mastery for Women - 12 Laws to Create Wealth Starting Today*.

Each chapter is dedicated to one of the 12 Laws, written by one of us, made rich by our own unique experiences. Each Law contains 3 action steps selected by the author as the best way for you to begin starting today!

When you apply the simple action steps you *will* create a successful business and a life you love living. When you follow the instructions given in each chapter you *will* succeed. You will master wealth and create a business and life filled with promise, while becoming wealthier than your wildest dreams.

Each author has a thriving, successful life of freedom and purpose built around the practice of the 12 Laws you find here. We have multiple businesses and lives we love living beyond measure and desire the very same for YOU! Our intention in writing this book is to share the powerful success principles and practices, empowering women everywhere to know and live Wealth Mastery. You have a dream and desire to be a woman of purpose, to build a business and life of freedom, success and fun and we are here to show you the way.

We are immensely grateful that you are holding this book in your hands. You are taking the first step in saying YES to be, do, have and give all that you dream in life and in a business you love.

Do not let your dreams die inside of you. Embrace your desires and make the very best of your beautiful, unique gifts and talents. As you are developing in this step-by-step process, you will watch them grow and expand into the visions and dreams you hold in your heart. Know that while you are on your journey, we are with you every step of the way. So now, let's begin.

Yours truly,

Paula Fellingham and The Four Dames, 2015

Table of Contents

Believe that being wealthy is not only possible; see it as a real part of your future.

Deciding to be wealthy is an extension of that belief. Once you steadfastly believe and decide, your subconscious mind will begin to make abundance a reality in your life.

~ Paula Fellingham

~*LAW ONE*~

DECIDE TO BE WEALTHY
Create and Maintain an Abundance Mindset

Paula Fellingham

As easy as this first Law seems, it is the number one reason most people fail to acquire wealth. They simply never decide to be wealthy.

Making that decision is, absolutely, within your power and it's easier than you may think. It begins with understanding the power of choice. The power we all have, every minute of every day, with every thought we think and every action we take.

Yes, "Decide to Be Wealthy" is the most important and also the easiest of all the 12 Laws. Napoleon Hill, in his book *Think and Grow Rich,* wrote, "...riches begin with a state of mind, with definiteness of purpose, with little or no hard work."

There is, within every human being, the belief that we can be more than we are. I'm confident you know that every success begins with our beliefs. It follows, then, that the first step to creating wealth must be a belief that we CAN be wealthy, and a decision to BE wealthy.

William James, whom many revere as the father of psychology, said, **"The greatest discovery of my generation is that human beings can alter their lives by altering their beliefs."**

My friends, within each one of us is a power we scarcely tap. This power has fueled heroic deeds since time began and has energized great inventors, artists and musicians throughout the ages. It's the exact same power available to each of us – every day of our lives. It is the power of belief.

What is a belief? It is a sense of certainty about something. For example, if you believe you're a good musician you think, "I feel certain that I'm a fine musician." And that sense of certainty helps you produce beautiful music. On the other hand, a negative belief works the same way. If you say, "I'm a terrible singer," you'll produce the results that validate your belief.

This applies perfectly to our beliefs around wealth and wealth creation. I believe, without a shadow of doubt that the very first step in creating anything of value in our lives begins with believing that we can.

Marcus Aurelius said, "A man's life is what his beliefs make of it."

Dale Carnegie taught, "Believe that you will succeed. Believe it firmly, and you will then do what is necessary to bring success about."

So many people go through life without ever consciously and deliberately choosing to be wealthy. And yet, if you ask them, they'll say that being wealthy is one of the things they want most in life. Sadly, however, they go through their entire lives wishing but never believing; wanting but never choosing; waiting but never deciding – truly deciding – to be wealthy.

Instead, they allow life, and others, to determine their destinies. They simply react to circumstances in their lives. They're not proactively moving forward, making decisions and directing their own paths.

Imagine a pilot coming over the intercom and announcing: "I have some bad news and some good news. The bad news is we've lost one engine and our direction finder. The good news is we have a tail wind and wherever we are going we're getting there at a rate of 600 miles an hour." People often fly along like that – directionless, but being pushed swiftly along by the winds of circumstances.

I love the story about the time Justice Oliver Wendell Holmes misplaced his ticket while traveling on a train. Watching him fumble through his belongings and pockets in growing frustration, the conductor said, "Don't worry about it, Mr. Holmes. I'm sure you have your ticket somewhere. If you don't find it during the trip, just mail it in to the railroad when you reach your destination." Holmes looked the conductor in the eye and said, "Young man, my problem is not finding my ticket. It's finding out where in the world I'm going!"

Where are you going?

I'd like to suggest that you choose wealth and move forward deliberately, taking the steps that lead to success found in this book we are providing for you, *12 Laws to Create Wealth, Starting Today.* I absolutely believe that when you live these Laws you will create wealth and amazing abundance.

I'd like to suggest that there are seven steps to achieve any goal. These are all predicated on your belief that you can, and will, be successful.

To align with our discussion about wealth, your decision to be wealthy is the goal we're focusing on here. However, these steps can be applied to any of your goals.

Your goal: Wealth Creation for You and Your Family.
Your belief: "I Can Create Great Wealth."
Your decision: "I Decide to Be Wealthy."
Your support: This book, other resources, your mentors (The Wealth Mastery Team: Paula, Patricia, Julie, Lynn and Marilyn).
Our "Wealth Help Line" – 866-GO WOMEN – or results@WealthMasteryForWomen.com

7 Steps to Get You There...

1. CHOOSE GREAT GOALS. You should choose only goals you deeply care about and are committed to achieving. Choose to be wealthy only if you deeply care about being wealthy and are committed to achieving financial abundance for yourself and your family.

The more deeply you are convinced of the absolute necessity of reaching your goal, the more tenacity you'll exert as you work toward it.

How do you decide to be wealthy?

- Go somewhere alone; do not be rushed.

- Think deeply and slowly about the decision to create wealth.

- Create detailed, visual pictures in your mind of your ideal self and your ideal life. "See yourself" wealthy. See your home; your car; your neighborhood; your ability to pay for things easily; your ability to give to others easily; your ability to help your loved ones and friends. Feel the peace of mind you have when you're out of debt completely. Feel the joy that comes from knowing you can lighten the loads of others. See and feel all these things in great detail, taking your time and enjoying the experience.

- Carefully consider where you want to be in ten years. Visualize it.

- Ask yourself, "What do I want to be doing in ten years? Who do I want to be with? What do I want to look like? What do I want my life to look like?"

- Then think about your life in five years...in one year...in six months...in one month.

- Use my "I Dr." 3-Step Formula:

  Identify your goal.
  Decide what your highest priorities are, your "first steps."
  Resolve to focus like a laser beam.

2. Write Your Goal in Detailed Specifics

This is of utmost importance. There was an experiment conducted in 1985 with 100 high school students who all decided on future goals.

Fifty of the students talked about their goals but never wrote them down.

Fifty students wrote their goals in specific terms and gave time limits.

Ten years later the students were questioned.

Of the fifty students who didn't write their goals down, 15% achieved them. Of those who wrote in specific details with time deadlines, 92% achieved their goals.

Give your mind a clearly defined goal it can envision and work toward.

3. Give Yourself a Time Limit

You want dreams with a deadline. Beside your goal, write WHEN you'll achieve the goal.

For some goals, you'll list the small steps you'll take on your way to reaching your goal. And you'll write an "achievement date" beside each one of the small steps.

Participate in the ACTION STEPS (below) on each of the 12 Laws.

4. Break Goals Into Small, Doable Steps

No matter how large the task, it is infinitely easier when broken down into daily tasks.

We help you with this throughout the book and especially in our "Wealth Mastery for Women Mentoring Program."

5. Consistently and Enthusiastically Take Action

"Nothing good or great can be done in the absence of enthusiasm."

Tom Peters

My friend, along your way to wealth you may encounter friends and family members who ridicule your efforts to acquire wealth. You may experience opposition. If so, remember that consistently and enthusiastically taking action – NO MATTER WHAT – is a key to your success.

This poem, written by the famous poet Edgar A. Guest, may help you maintain your enthusiasm.

<u>It Couldn't Be Done</u>

Somebody said that it couldn't be done,
But he with a chuckle replied,
"Maybe it couldn't," but he would be one
Who wouldn't say so till he tried.
So he buckled right in with the trace of a grin
On his face. If he worried, he hid it.
He started to sing as he tackled the thing
That couldn't be done, and he did it!
Somebody scoffed, "Oh, you'll never do that;
At least no one has ever done it;"

But he took off his coat and he took off his hat,
And the first thing we knew he'd begun it!
With a lift of his chin and a bit of a grin,
Without any doubting or quiddit,
He started to sing as he tackled the thing
That couldn't be done, and he did it!
There are thousands to tell you it cannot be done,
There are thousands to prophesy failure;
There are thousands to point out to you, one by one,
The dangers that await to assail you.
But just buckle in with a bit of a grin,
Just take off your coat and go to it;
Just start to sing as you tackle the thing
That "cannot be done" and you'll do it!

6. Notice What's Working (or not) and Reward Yourself Along the Way

<u>Positive reinforcement is the best way to learn</u>!

Immediately reinforce the slightest progress. The moment you achieve one of your smaller goals along the way to creating wealth, give yourself a reward!

7. Continue to Make Course Corrections Until You Achieve

All airplane pilots, CEOs and ship captains understand this: staying on course as you progress toward your goal requires course corrections. From time to time, as you move toward your goal, you'll veer a little to the right or to the left because distractions and obstacles are inevitable. Count on them; don't let them discourage you. Make course corrections and get back in the groove.

Those are the seven steps to successful goal achievement.

So now that you know your goal – to create wealth starting today – you can begin by simply saying, in your heart and aloud (loud and strong), "I decide to be wealthy." These words, repeated frequently and believed sincerely, carry with them a force that can influence the subconscious mind to bring about your declaration and desire.

Once you have decided something, firmly and with no reservation, your subconscious mind will begin to create the reality necessary to bring to pass exactly what you declare and desire.

And finally, I'll lovingly remind you of three things. First, when choosing to be wealthy, choose also to release yourself from any limiting beliefs, from all old patterns that do not serve you well, and from every reason why you cannot live the life you love.

Second, as you are developing an abundance mindset, it is important to recognize and be thankful for the great wealth of abundance that is already yours. God has supplied everything necessary to bless and prosper you. Part of your job is to recognize and be sincerely grateful for the blessings you now enjoy. For it is through gratitude that abundance is born. The more grateful you are, the more abundance you attract.

And third, believe that being wealthy is not only possible; see it as a real part of your future. Your decision to be wealthy is an extension of that belief. Once you steadfastly believe and decide, your subconscious mind will begin to make wealth and abundance a reality in your life.

LAW ONE - ACTION STEPS

DECIDE TO BE WEALTHY

Create and Maintain an Abundance Mindset

Action Steps

1. Say aloud, "I decide to be wealthy" and talk to a trusted friend or family member about how you've decided to be wealthy, and how you're going to create wealth. On paper write, "I decide to be wealthy" then sign your name big and bold.

2. Watch the "Decide to Be Wealthy" video on www.WealthMasteryforWomen.com.

3. When a negative thought around this decision appears, say to yourself, "Stop. The truth is, I decide to be wealthy." You may want to create a personal mantra such as, "I receive increased love, increased prosperity, and increased success in every area of my life as I help others do the same."

Today is the first day of the rest of your life!   The only question is…

What will you create?

~ Patricia Barnett

~*LAW TWO*~

UNDERSTAND HOW TO BE WEALTHY

Create a Clear Vision and Compelling "Why?"

Patricia Barnett

"Without a vision, the people perish."

– Proverbs 29:18

So now that you have decided to be wealthy, let's dive deeper into a process that can help you create wealth easier, quicker, faster and with a whole lot of FUN!

The first thing many people think of when they hear the word "wealth" is money itself. While it is a fact that money is part of being wealthy, there are many forms in which wealth is created in our lives. Being diagnosed with a life-threatening disease many years ago, I became very aware that health is actually our very first wealth. Without my life, having all of the money in the world would not have made much difference. And yet, in our lives today, cash flow, assets and funds are essential in creating our dreams and living our very best lives. In addition to health, wealth comes to us in other treasures such as valued relationships, time freedom and a wealth of information. Ideas, consciousness and prosperity as well as peace, joy and happiness are also signs of wealth.

I believe that with the correct tools, knowing how to use them properly and then applying these tools in a certain way, you can create literally A-N-Y-T-H-I-N-G! The most important tool to know and to use next in the process of Wealth Mastery is defining, designing and refining the wealth you would love to create.

There is something that is seeking to be created by you. And in this "something" it is most likely what you are here to create. The "something" speaks to each of us through the desires or discontents of our hearts and in our lives. You may have an idea of something you would love to create specifically, or you have chosen to read this book in order to find the "true" wealth that resides within you. Either way, I am going to invite you to really "take the lid off" of your thinking to then tap into the reservoir of possibilities for your future. Rather than moving right into the "Vision Process" for the goals you have currently, I invite you to take a moment for a very fun and enlightening exercise to discover all of the ways you would love to experience true abundance and wealth in your life in addition to money itself.

This activity of generating ideas has many names. Some call it a "bucket list," others call it "brainstorming," and still others refer to it as a "brain dump." It is the process of listing all that you would love to BE, DO, HAVE, GIVE and/or CREATE in your life. We like to refer to it as your "Love List." The beauty in this process is that much may be revealed to you. Some ideas that you know you would love, others you may have forgotten, or some you were not aware of at all. It is easy, it is FUN, and it will reveal exactly how you would love wealth to show up in your life.

Take a few moments to begin this exercise now. You'll need a notebook (make a chart like the graph on the following page) and a few quiet moments by yourself. Close your eyes and take several deep breaths to relax yourself. As you find a deeper level of relaxation, ask yourself this question... "Who would I love to BE in my life?" Allow thoughts to come to you and as they do, begin to write them in your notebook. When you have finished writing those thoughts, close your eyes again, take a breath, and ask the next question: "What would I love to DO in my life?" Continue this process until you have asked yourself the following five questions:

1. "Who would I love to be in my life?"
2. "What would I love to do in my life?"
3. "What would I love to have in my life?"
4. "What would I love to give in my life?"
5. "What would I love to create in my life?"

BE	DO	HAVE	GIVE	CREATE
Best Selling Author	Travel to Europe	Home by the Ocean	My Time to Support Women	Thriving Speaking and Coaching Business
1.				
2.				
3.				
4.				

5.				
6.				
7.				
8.				

For the mere fact that you asked these questions and have completed this exercise, sometimes even greater ideas will begin to flow to you over the next minutes, hours, days or even weeks. You have opened the channel of ideas and possibilities to come to you. The key is to continue to add to your list, writing the ideas as quickly as they come to you.

One day a prospective client came to me asking for help in increasing her income in a certain business she was affiliated. She said, "I want to earn significantly more money; yet I can't quite figure out why others are always succeeding and I am not." After identifying her personal "Love List" it became so clear; this client was not in a business that was in alignment with what she desired *to be, do, have, give* or *create*. Upon shifting her focus to what she *did* love, she immediately increased her earnings, increased her joy, improved her health and even opened to a whole lot more fun in her life. Truly, ideas are the first form of currency in creating wealth.

A quick note: sometimes, during this exercise, fear may show up as the thought "I have no idea what I would love." If this happens, simply begin with the things you know you would love for sure. Other times, fear will show up as the "inner critic," saying things like, "Are you kidding yourself?" "You could never do that!" or "Who are you to think you could be, do or have that?" If this happens, simply press pause on those thoughts. This exercise is designed to stretch your imagination and to expand your awareness of the dreams that reside within you.

Once you have "turned up the volume" of the possibilities for your life, it can be very tempting to want to take immediate action to achieve *all* of them at once. This is where the art of focused attention is important in producing real results most effectively. I've heard it said that diffused light, lights up a room (in the example of a light bulb). Focused light, however, can cut through steel (think laser beam). The same is true for our attention and focus. As women, we have been led to believe that "doing it all at once" (multitasking) gets more things done quicker. This concept could not be further from the truth. The fact is by focusing our attention on fewer items at one time and in completing each before going onto the next, we are more productive with less effort and in less time.

As you look at all of the items for achievement on your "Love List," the question is this, which do you love most? Choose 5 to 10 of the items from your list that you would LOVE to accomplish within the next 3 years. If you are feeling like there is no way you could choose only 5 or 10 items, relax. Simply take a few deep breaths and ask, "What am I sure I would love to accomplish in the next three years?" and then listen. It is as if your dreams will speak to you. Next, let's take it one step further and list your top 5 *LOVES* below:

1. _____

   _____

2. _____

   _____

3. _____

   _____

4. _____

   _____

5. _____

   _____

For many, money is at the top of the list. And yet, very rarely, if ever, is *money* actually what is truly desired. Allow me to explain. Recently, I was speaking with my niece, Ashley, about earning money. She told me she was very interested in earning money, $200 to be exact. Ashley said, "Aunt Patricia, I am really motivated to earn this money as soon as possible." I shared with my niece the same idea I am sharing with you here. I said, "Ashley, it is not really the money that is motivating you..." Before I could finish Ashley said emphatically, "Oh yes, money motivates *me!*" Then I asked *why* she was so interested in the money. Ashley proceeded to tell me her "Why." She desired money to buy the newest, latest and greatest, state of the art cell phone that would allow her more freedom and FUN. The fun part for me is that it did not take Ashley long to see that it was the FREEDOM the cell phone would provide that was her true motivation.

And the same thing is true for you too...

The next step in "turning up the volume" in achieving your goals is to find *your* "Why?" For example, maybe one of your Top 5 Goals is to be healthy, lean, fit or to have more energy. All are great goals; however, the next question is *"Why?"* Why would you love more energy? What would you do with it if you had it? If your goal is money or financial freedom then ask yourself, *"Why* would you love this?" What will you do with the freedom of finances? If you desire more love in your life, you guessed it, the question is, *"Why?"* What would that mean to you and how would your life be different?

Next, list the "Why's" for your Top 5 Goals.

1. Why? _____

_____

_____

2. Why? _____

_____

_____

3. Why? _____

_____

_____

4. Why? _____

_____

_____

5. Why? _____

_____

_____

When we get really good at asking and answering the question of *"Why?"*, it is as if the volume of our goals is turned up once again and we actually become tuned into the results at a more elevated and emotional level. It is at this level where creating your vision has the most power to support you in achieving your goals and dreams. Just as my niece became enthused by speaking of her new cell phone, pictures began to surface in her mind (and in mine too) of what it would look like when she had her desire in hand. The same is true for you. In answering your "Why" questions above, it is most likely that a vision came to your mind while pondering the answer to the *"Why?"* question as well.

The reason having an image of your desired goal is so important in the "Vision Process" is because our minds think in pictures. It is said, "Without vision the people perish." This is absolutely the truth and yet in achieving results it is the specificity of the vision where the power resides. For a moment, bring to mind one of the visions that came to mind while working on the list above. In your mind it might look like a photo or snapshot of the experience you'd love. It might even look like an entire movie. The key to writing a vision is to describe what it is you are seeing in your mind in detail. Using all of your five senses describe your vision. What does it look like? Are there any sounds or smells? What do you feel? Maybe you are eating a meal in your vision; if so what does it taste like?

> **"To be wealthy, we must *BE* wealthy."**
>
> ~ Patricia Barnett

The specificity of each of your Top 5 Goals is important because the more you internalize the experience *while* taking actions to achieve your results, the more you become like a magnet making welcome all of the resources necessary to achieve your goals. The magnet I am referring to actually resides within you and is called your personal belief system. The truth is that we will never be able to outperform our own self-image. First build the image in your mind of your desired goal. Next, live *from* that image daily, *while* taking appropriate action. Your belief system will grow and your results will follow. This is the succeeding step in creating wealth and where life gets a whole lot easier and way more FUN!

One day while speaking at a conference for women, I shared this "Vision Process" concept and additional ways to move through the barriers that show up when creating results and achieving goals and dreams. I used the example of traveling to New York City. In the example I painted the picture of the specifics of what my trip to New York City would look like. I shared in great detail the five-star accommodations at the Plaza Hotel, fine dining, shopping and Broadway shows. After sharing this "vision" I asked, "So, who would like to go with me?" Many hands went up and one woman stood up in the crowd and said, "I would! It has been *my lifelong dream* to live in New York City!" After the conference, we began working together and within six months she had moved all the way across the country and was living her dreams in New York City. This is what's possible when applying the 12 Laws. Whether it is your health, your wealth, your relationships or your work in the world, knowing what you would love and having a clear vision of it is of utmost importance.

You are now ready to take your goal achievement to the next level – creating your vision. Describe below what the vision for your Top 5 Goals looks like *and* feels like:

#1

_____

_____

_____

_____

_____

#2

_____

_____

_____

_____

#3

_____

_____

_____

_____

#4

_____

_____

_____

_____

#5

_____

_____

_____

_____

LAW TWO - ACTION STEPS

UNDERSTAND HOW TO BE WEALTHY

Create a Clear Vision and Compelling "Why?"

Action Steps:

1. List your Top 5 Goals.

2. For each of your Top 5 Goals write a sentence explaining your "Why?"

3. Describe in detail what your ideal life looks like when your Top 5 Goals are achieved.

As a special gift to support you in writing your vision and to learn more about the vision process please review:

The Vital 7 - Essential Elements to Create a Vision that Works for YOU!

www.PatriciaBarnett.com/TheVital7

Your wealth within includes your ability to love, your values, skills and talents. Use them to lift others, and the Law of Reciprocity will return to you wealth beyond measure.

~ Paula Fellingham

~LAW THREE~

IDENTIFY YOUR WEALTH WITHIN
Assess Your Unique Strengths and Wins!

Paula Fellingham

I'll begin Law Three with one of my favorite stories. This life-changing story reminds us of our priceless worth.

There was once an Indian farmer named Ali Hafid who could neither read nor write, but who was fortunate enough to have his own farm, a fine wife, and a good family.

One day a traveling monk came to Hafid and told him about a marvelous discovery recently made of a jewel called a diamond.

The story so caught the imagination of Ali Hafid that he sold his farm and house and left his wife and family to search for diamonds. He traveled far and wide searching, but never found the precious stones. Finally, broken in body and spirit, having exhausted his funds in his fruitless search, he cast himself into the sea and drowned.

About that time the monk came through the village again and stopped at the farm formerly owned by Hafid. There on the mantel he saw a lovely diamond.

"I see Ali found his diamond," he said, pointing to the stone.

"Oh, Ali sold me his farm," said the new owner, "and that stone is just a pretty rock I found down in the streambed as I watered my sheep."

"Show me the place," said the monk, and the man led him to the stream.

There, in the gravel bottom of the streambed, they found one diamond after another. A further search showed the whole farm contained diamonds, even in the dirt floor in the cellar of the house. The story claims that thus the rich Golconda diamond field was discovered. There beneath his very feet was the fortune for which Ali Hafid gave his life in a fruitless search.

The lesson?

The greatest treasure you'll ever find lies within you. Don't fall into the trap of neglecting to discover that life's greatest prize is within.

You are priceless.

You are of infinite worth.

Your life is precious and extremely valuable.

My friends, we all have unique gifts and talents, and skills we can use to help improve our own lives and the lives of others. Some people choose to develop their talents in such ways that they touch the hearts and change the lives of millions worldwide.

Others choose to live smaller lives, but they use their talents and skills in profoundly significant ways that forever change the lives of those in their circles of influence. Sometimes many generations are blessed because kind people generously share their special gifts with no thought of reward.

One way is not better than another. The important thing to know is that we are all children of God and we all have great wealth within.

The wise identify their gifts, develop them and share them in a way that expands what is good and creates abundance and joy wherever they go.

Mother Teresa said, "Let no one ever come to you without leaving better and happier."

As we discover, develop and share our talents we can more successfully give to others in meaningful, life-changing ways.

It begins with asking these questions, which I invite you to take a moment and do.

What are my unique gifts?

What is my "wealth within"?

How can I best develop my gifts?

How can I most effectively share my gifts with others?

After working with women in many nations for over 30 years, one of the universal truths I've learned is that most women lack confidence and they have a difficult time truly loving themselves.

Women are natural nurturers and givers, but confidently declaring that they're talented and gifted – with great value to share with others – is difficult for most women.

It's important, however, to ask ourselves the question, "How can we fully love others if we don't fully love ourselves?" I would like to suggest that you begin by confidently declaring (to yourself) that although you're trying to improve every day, you are "enough" today...just the way you are.

My friend, what do you see, right now, in your "self mirror"?

I believe that what you think of yourself determines your success boundaries and sets your limits.

By improving your self-image, you expand your boundaries and extend your limits.

Where is your "self-picture" and who creates it?

It's in your mind, and you do.

Your brain is a marvelous mechanism that works for your success or for your failure. Since you're the operator, the outcome depends on your skills. Are you in control? Do you direct and carefully maneuver your thoughts so that you focus on your goals – steering straight toward them as you power along life's highway? Or are you out of control, frequently allowing negative and destructive thoughts to take the wheel?
Know, without a doubt, that you can drive your thoughts, words and actions in the direction of high achievement, every day. And with the right tools and consistent effort, you can steer yourself toward previously unimagined joy and unattainable success.

How did you learn that you're good at some things and not good at others? You experienced success and failure from your earliest years and you built beliefs about yourself based on these experiences, and on the way people reacted to you.

For example, during your first years at school, if you excelled in art, your work was praised. If you repeatedly bungled math problems, you were reproved. You learned, from experience and other people's reactions, that you were a good artist and a bad mathematician. Consciously and unconsciously, you developed a self-picture from your experiences and the input of others.

If you have a poor self-image in any area of your life because of past negative experiences, there is good news! You can improve your self-image by creating new, positive experiences to replace the old ones.

Author Harry Fosdick wrote, "Great living starts with a pix held in your imagination of what you would like to do or be."

You see, the very nature of the human brain and nervous system allows you to literally *create experiences* in your mind. Experimental and clinical psychologists have proven:

1. The nervous system cannot tell the difference between an ACTUAL experience and an experience IMAGINED IN GREAT DETAIL.

2. Your nervous system reacts obediently to what you think or imagine to be true – whether it's actually true or not. In other words, people always feel, act and behave according to what they *imagine to be true* about themselves and their circumstances.

Many studies have proven that every accomplishment is first created in our imagination. For example:

- Gymnastics champion Mary Lou Retton has described how she rehearsed every routine in her mind, visualizing every step, every leap and turn, every hand placement before putting her body through the actual performance.
- Juliet McComas, concert pianist, said, "If I visualize the keyboard, I can practice in an airport or at my kitchen table. It's just as useful as actual practice."
- Arnold Schwarzenegger said, "As long as the mind can envision the fact that you can do something, you can. I visualized myself being there already – having achieved the goal already."

I'd like to suggest four things you can do to "see yourself" succeed:

1. Each day take 5 minutes and relax – close your eyes. Create a mental motion picture of yourself, as you would like to be. Imagine, in great detail, your "best self." Imagine your face radiant and smiling; your body at its optimum shape and fitness level; your clothes well-fitting and nice. Imagine (in great detail) doing something extremely well that you enjoy doing.

   Maxwell Maltz, author of *Psycho Cybernetics,* said, "Imagine how you would feel if you were already the sort of personality you want to be."

2. As you go through your day, when life becomes overwhelming and you need a mental break, take a mini vacation in your mind. This is easily done with practice.

You simply create in your mind a wonderful place where you're very happy. For some this is an exquisitely decorated palace; for others it's a walk along a warm, clean, sandy beach with someone they love. For still others it's a beautiful room with a large, comfortable bed...and a big window looking out onto a pond and flower garden.

Wherever you go in your mind, you need to see that place in great detail. Touch the palace walls, smell the ocean, feel the soft pillow on the bed. Are you with me here? Can you visualize?

Dr. Norman Vincent Peale wrote, "Fill your mind with all peaceful experiences possible, then make planned and deliberate excursions to them in memory."

3. A third way you can use this marvelous tool of visualization is to release yourself from damaging beliefs from the past or to heal yourself from past pain.

    Everyone who has experienced emotional pain and heartache knows that it is very real and extraordinarily difficult to forget. Although you can't erase the past, you can help yourself heal with visualization. Here's how: When a painful memory forces itself into your mind, **label** it with "That hurt" (because it did) and then **replace** it with a thought about how the person SHOULD HAVE ACTED. Instead of letting your mind replay the experience as it was, imagine how it should have been.

4. A fourth way you can use visualization is to imagine yourself into the future, performing successfully: giving a presentation, achieving a goal, being patient/kind/ forgiving, etc.

Again, you create mental pictures in your mind – in great detail. You imagine every part of the experience like this: I think to myself,

I'm going to give this presentation to my department in twenty-four hours. I've prepared well; I know the material. I will imagine what it will be like.

I'm going to get up tomorrow morning with a positive, upbeat attitude and look forward to the presentation. I'll put on my navy blue suit, my hair will look great and I'll feel really good about my appearance.

I can see myself right now...yeah, I look good! After a healthful breakfast, I'll go through the presentation highlights out loud, so it will be on the tip of my tongue. Then I'll take my briefcase and drive to work calmly because I've left plenty of time to get there.
As soon as I get to work I'll email the department and remind them of the meeting. I'll answer my mail and pick up my presentation handouts. On the way to the meeting I'll get a drink of water, and then confidently open the door of the boardroom. Inside I see my colleagues looking at me with admiration and respect. I go to the front of the room and lay out my materials.
I stand in front of the group confidently – with my shoulders back and smiling...anxious to begin. As I present I am articulate and witty. I remember to speak slowly enough to be understood, and I patiently answer every question. My co-workers are interested in my information and enjoy the meeting.

Afterwards I thank them for their interest and participation and I graciously accept their compliments.

Do you see how it works?

Now what if the unexpected happens – a flat tire, the computers are down, or a co-worker is sarcastic during your presentation?

You'll be gracious and calm no matter what happens because you understand that neither other people nor your circumstances can determine your reactions.

Dr. Harry Fosdick said, "Hold a picture of yourself long and steadily enough in your mind's eye and you will be drawn toward it. Picture yourself vividly as defeated and that alone will make victory impossible. Picture yourself vividly as winning and that alone will contribute immeasurably to success."

Through the years I've shared this next story with thousands, and it always resonates well.

One summer during the 1950s a bright Stanford College student named Henry Eyring labored over a difficult physics problem. Finally, he decided to ask his father for help. This young man's father was not just any ordinary guy – he was a Nobel prize–winning scientist.

As the wise scientist studied his son's problem he asked, "Isn't this problem similar to one that we worked on last week?" Young Eyring answered, "Yes, I guess so..." And his father then asked, "Well, what have you been thinking about this week...I mean when you were walking along, or in the shower, or driving? Weren't you thinking about this problem?" His son admitted that no, he didn't think about the problem at all. The brilliant father then asked a question which his son never, ever forgot. He said,

"Son, what do you think about when you don't *have* to think about anything?"

Henry admitted that he didn't think about science. And then, with a sad expression on his face, the Nobel prize winner remarked, "Then you better not be a scientist. You should go into whatever field you think about when you don't have to think about anything."

I would like to ask you that same question. "What do you think about when you don't *have* to think about anything?" Whatever you think about when you don't have to think about anything could be the key to showing you what your gifts are, and how you could use them to create a meaningful, joy-filled life.

In the Theater of Your Mind you can play whatever scenes you choose. What I'm suggesting is that you steer your thoughts down positive paths during times when you don't *have* to think about anything.

As we leave Law #3, I'd like to share a wonderful story told by Rachel Naomi Remen, MD. She's the author of the outstanding book *My Grandfather's Blessings* (Penguin Putnam, NY, 2000, pg. 120,121).

"Years ago, I cared for a desperately sick two-year-old boy with bacterial meningitis. Deeply unconscious, Ricardo lay in a nest of IV lines and monitor cords, his tiny body almost hidden by the technology that supported and documented his struggle to live.

"His mother, a slight Filipina woman, sat at the foot of his bed day after day. She even slept there, sitting in her chair and leaning forward across the mattress. Whenever any of us came to examine Ricardo or draw blood from him, we would find her there, often with her eyes closed, one hand under her baby's blanket. She was holding on to his foot.

"After he began to recover and the life-support equipment was withdrawn, I asked her about this. She smiled and looked away, a little embarrassed. But she told me that for all those days she had felt that his life depended on her holding on to his foot. Moved, I asked her what had been going on in her mind all that time. Had she been praying for his recovery? No, she told me, while she was holding his foot, she would just close her eyes and dream her dreams for him.

"Day after day she would watch him grow up. She would imagine taking him to his first day of school, see him learning to read and to write and play ball, sit in church at his first communion, watch him graduate from high school, dance at his wedding. She would imagine him as the father of her grandchild. Over and over and over again. She flushed slightly. 'Perhaps,' she told me, 'it made a difference.'"

Dr. Remen then added, "Sometimes we may strengthen the life in others when we have an image of the future and hold on to it fiercely, much as Ricardo's mother did."

When you imagine positive scenes, over and over in your mind, your confidence level will increase, your performance will improve, and you will be able to act AS IF you already are the person you want to become.

Now, seriously ask yourself this question again.

"What is my wealth within?"

Perhaps these questions and ideas will help you answer that question...

What do you love to do that when you are doing it, time flies by?

When you lean into what gives you life and do what you love doing, identifying your "golden nuggets within" becomes easier.

When creating an inventory of your wealth within, begin where you are, with what you have right now.

Identify your current assets; list them all.

What are your talents?

Who are your contacts?

What resources are available to you now?

What is your uniqueness?

What are your very best qualities and finest skills?

Reflect on your past and shine a light on all of your successes and wins. Highlight the moments of joy and what brought you the most happiness.

Having clarity regarding your achievements will aid you in your self-discovery and help you identify your inner strengths. Listen to your inner calling and intuition.

Every human has the exact amount of life force within. No one has less; no one has more. It is in the identifying of the immense amount of unlimited potential that resides in you that will awaken you to your wealth within.

Identify Your Wealth Within; Your Unique Strengths and WINS!

Action Steps

1. Identify your gifts and talents by writing an inventory list of what you love to do and what you excel in.

2. List 10 past successes and WINS!

3. On a scale of 1 to 5 (1 is "poor" and 5 is "excellent") rate your current "wealth" in these areas:

❖ Physical Well-Being   _____

❖ Emotional Well-Being   _____

❖ Mental Gifts   _____

❖ Social Talents   _____

❖ Financial Strengths   _____

❖ Family Relationships   _____

❖ Friend Relationships   _____

❖ Business Contacts   _____

❖ Business Resources   _____

❖ Creative Ideas   _____

❖ Other Gifts – add here: _____

This activity is designed to help you evaluate your strengths and weaknesses. You can more easily assess your "wealth within" when you rate yourself this way. Be kind and generous (to yourself) as you do this. Also, know that we are here to help you, every step of the way, towards Wealth Mastery and Total Life Excellence.

LAW THREE - ACTION STEPS

IDENTIFY YOUR WEALTH WITHIN

Assess Your Unique Strengths and Wins!

Action Steps:

1. Identify your "wealth within" by answering the questions asked in this Law Three chapter.

2. Create a list of all your past successes and WINS!

3. Identify and list your current wealth in the areas of health, finance, relationships, contacts, resources, friends and ideas (above).

4. Share (written or aloud) your dream/goal of how you can use your strengths/assets to live a life of abundance and complete fulfillment/service to others/global legacy.

Look around you. You've created the world that you believe you deserve.

Aspire to love yourself first.

~ Marilyn Macha

~*LAW FOUR*~

LOOK, LEARN AND DISCOVER
Be Curious, Be Creative and Do Your Research

Marilyn Macha

"It's not what you look at that matters, it's what you see."

–Henry David Thoreau

I have been, and continue to be, blessed. We all are, when we look for blessings. Blessings are always there. We are learning to open our eyes to see them. And the law of vibration, the laws of physics, have proven that what you look for, where you put your attention, is what you will have more of. It's physics. How abundant are we willing to be? As Paula referenced in Law One, DECIDE to be wealthy and watch what thoughts begin to show up. Perhaps: "You don't deserve it." "Who do you think you are?" "It would take too much work; it won't last anyway..." When we decide to be wealthy (in body, mind and soul) all that has been holding us back will rear its head and try to stop you. That's normal; it's called survival – and that's why you must desire to be wealthy more than you want the status quo. It's up to you.

I've been asked frequently, "How did you 'do it'? How did you start a business, run a business and sell that business for a profit? What made you think that you even could?" Well, all that I originally "saw" was to prove that I could be independent AND, as a single mom, take care of my small son and myself. It was, as Napoleon Hill calls it, a Burning Desire.

And that's the beginning: LOOK—look at what you would love your life to look like—and then, SEE what there is to do about that. It starts with a thought, a desire and a vision, what your mind can SEE.

So to "look" is the first step; to be willing to look at what you would love. Seeing something available will naturally be the next view. You will see yourself in a particular home, relationship, office, perhaps at a computer or calling on prospects, receiving an award, holding someone's hand...

Take a moment now to look at what you would love. See your body, your vitality in performance; see yourself interacting in loving relationships; see yourself interacting, contributing to others. Is it at the Performing Arts Center, as a contributor of the symphony? Is it being a coach on your child's softball team? Is it flying to Guatemala as part of a volunteer medical group? How would you love your life to look? Where are you traveling? Are you skiing? At the spa? Climbing the mountains of Sedona?

Be bold! Let your imagination become the electricity that lights up your life!!

Now that we're "looking," it's important to see the difference between "look" and "see"; they are distinct. The difference between look and see takes an awareness. When we "look" out into the world, we "see" what our thinking from the past tells us to see. It takes a curiosity to begin to discover what "I am seeing." Is it the truth for me? Is it really the truth, or is it my interpretation? Would someone else see something different? If I look out my front window and it's raining, do I see adversity, something that shouldn't be happening, or do I see a cleansing shower bringing a smile to my face and a sense of all is right with the world?

Our relationship with money (which most of us equate to "wealth") is like that, too. What do you tell yourself about money? How much can you have? How easy will you allow your life to be? What is money for? Is it there to share, to hoard, to fear its lack? Begin to get curious of your story about money, and ask perhaps a new question as to what you see as its contribution to support you in life.

Write down the following questions and spend some quiet time pondering your insight.

"What story do I tell myself about money? What's important to me about money?"

Write down what comes up for you. Look at what you truly "see" about money in your life. It was a very good exercise for me in expanding my relationship with money and the good that I will allow into my life...yes, what I will allow into my life. There is abundance everywhere and it is up to me if I allow something wonderful "in." Ponder that thought, also. Abundance is already showing up; you might be experiencing an abundance of debt, struggle or low income. In this very moment there is an abundance of prosperity, ease and significant income. We are always experiencing abundance of "something." What would you love to experience?

The word WEALTH is a thirteenth-century Old English word

meaning well-being and happiness. Interesting, isn't that? Over the last seven-plus centuries we have morphed the word into meaning "lots of money"...but WEALTH means an abundance of what makes our lives peaceful, fluid, joyous, filled with grace. WEALTH means a body that can enjoy all of the beauty of life.

We have been born to discover our essence, and as human beings we begin to learn about that mostly through adversity and challenges. We have a choice in every situation, every condition, every circumstance, but only if we look – and can see that "I <u>do</u> have a choice. I can be upset, angry with a situation, or I can choose to "be the woman," or "be the man" who makes a difference in that situation.

This takes practice, and it takes support. There's plenty of "support" to have life stay the same, to think that there is so much to fear, to worry about. Just turn on the news to confirm that point, or listen to conversations in a restaurant, on the street, at the cleaners – everywhere!

But where's the voice, the conversation that "Life is awesome!" That I have so many blessings, so many more blessings than difficulties – LOOK – discover them – give that discovery precedence and not what the media says, not what your neighbor says, or a frightened friend says how life *is*. You can support them without folding into their perception of what is happening.

Look! Learn ways, learn of groups, and learn what works for you to discover the abundance that is already yours! When you look for the good, the blessings, the support that is there already in that particular arena, you will find it. It's like the Google box on your computer. Ask the question and Google will search for everything in answer to THAT question. If you look for the blessings, you will find them; if you look for what is "wrong," you will find that! You will get more of what you concentrate on, where your thinking is. Take a LOOK and SEE the abundance in your life. That small, yet mighty observation brings more abundance, more wealth into your reality.

What if, in getting in touch with our desires, what we would love, we then discover that our desires actually fulfill an innate purpose for our life? What if we then begin to create situations, conversations, meetings that support what actually inspires our happiness and satisfaction? Once we begin to look – and see newly – we can begin to take action steps, design a strategy to research what we don't know that would move us into a job we would love, a partnership, an investment strategy, a home purchase. Research, believe, ask experts, get curious, ask questions (How does that work? Where would I begin?) Get curious! You can even Google questions that come to mind. Interview for jobs just for the experience and to see in what activities you would love to engage! Attend a class on making a good first impression. All of these inquiries are steps in becoming wealthy!

If and when you think that you very well could be (or are) creative or know creative people and are willing to take the steps that those thoughts provide, then you will begin to have even more ideas to begin your own wealth design.

A person who is wealthy acts wealthy, thinks wealthy thoughts, and thinks empowering thoughts that make a difference for themselves and for others. So how do you "act" wealthy? How do you "think" wealthy thoughts? The first thing to do is to "see" what you ARE thinking; and if you're not getting the results you want, remind yourself that they are YOUR results and you can do something about it. To think new thoughts requires that you notice what you are thinking, get support from someone who is getting the results in their life and be willing to consciously choose new thoughts.

Another thought to add is to make sure that the wealth you are seeking is not for you alone. What difference do you want to make with the wealth that is on its way to you? Steve Jobs made a difference in his own life, but he made a difference in all of our lives. Your contribution will make a difference when you see the difference that it can make in the lives of others (and in your life, of course!).

A person who wants to be wealthy must begin by "seeing" where she already is wealthy. Let me say that again. A person who wants to BE wealthy must begin by seeing where she already IS wealthy! See the abundance of color around you, the wealth of running water, the number of books that you own, the comfortable bed or soft pillow that you sleep on. Look for things that show you that you are already wealthy, abundant in life with things that you love. That energy, that thinking will bring more of wealth and things that you love, toward you. Then using our senses, especially our vision, to see in physical reality (in our mind first) where we are already wealthy, our imagination and intuition are triggered and the focus then becomes expansive.

To support this expansiveness consider creating a vision board. Cut pictures out of magazines; surround yourself with ideas, pictures, people who believe in the natural expansion of more (including more money, more time, more love, and more joy – but not just for "the sake of more"). Earl Nightingale defined success as "the progressive realization of a worthy goal". Making progress toward the life that you imagine, living a life of *more*, is a worthy goal. Dream big dreams. Allow many ideas and visions to come to you. Imagine and believe and be grateful! As you become aware of more ideas that light you up, you will begin to see that the ideas become more expansive themselves and they become about contributing to others, as well. You will eventually advance beyond what you might consider initially, as self-serving ideas, and you will see the good in the ideas for others. Then you are truly on your way!

It may mean that you want to start your own business. When I became an independent contractor in the investment world, all that I wanted to do in the beginning was to make money to support my son and me, to look good in the world and to do a good job for my clients. And then my vision began to grow as I gained confidence and created my own internal questions, ones that would forward me: Who am I becoming? What is my purpose here? What lights me up? And I spoke with people who were already successful, in my opinion, in that industry. Ask, ask, ask...and learn from others.

As you begin to discover who you really are: someone capable, creative, curious, willing to succeed, opportunities and "chance" meetings will happen over and over. You will be introduced to someone, for example, who wants to introduce you to someone who is exactly your perfect client. You will begin to see opportunities that you couldn't see before. Many people neglect to identify a willingness to succeed...it is paramount! Ask yourself the question, "Am I willing to succeed?" And then tell yourself the truth! As you begin to discover a more capable, successful, creative woman living within, you will begin to see more for yourself, more opportunities and you see more clearly those things that you desire and that you want to contribute. Keep asking yourself questions, but make sure they are questions that forward you, not a question like "Can I do this?" For example, more deliberate questions could be "Am I willing to do this? Does this light me up? Does it move me toward my dream? (Be very clear about what your 'dream' looks like.) To whom would I speak to learn more about this?"

This is simple work...not necessarily easy, but simple.

When you know WHY you want to succeed, why you want to feel free, you will find support daily. And it takes YOU to take the action steps. It takes YOU to seek your own truth and discover who you really are and what you would love. It must start from the inside. And then you will SEE what the next step is to take. Remember to research (go to the Google box), question, discover, be willing to look to SEE yourself and any challenge newly. Everything, everything is in your favor if you can look with new eyes to SEE the gift, the learning, the opportunity. Seek support, whether it be a mentor, a coach, a placement agency, a support group. You CAN do this. If I can do it, YOU can. Are you willing?

LAW FOUR - ACTION STEPS

LOOK, LEARN AND DISCOVER

Be Curious, Be Creative and Do Your Research

Action Steps

1. Look – Look at what you would love your life to look like – and then SEE what to do about it. Educate yourself: Internet, books and magazines, seminars, interviews. Research what others are doing in the field that you love and then ask yourself, "What would I do in this situation? What could I do in addition to what I'm already doing?"

2. Learn – Create a list of questions, then speak with people who are doing what you want to do. Ask, ask, ask...and learn from others. Design the questions around what you would love to know!

3. Discover – Seek the truth. Learn the true profit potential of your (future) business. Research real-world examples; do your due diligence carefully. And discover who you really are, someone capable, someone creative, someone curious, someone willing to succeed! You will attract people just like you to support you. Make sure that you are being the person that you would love to be supported by.

Behind every truly successful businesswoman, you will find a WINNING team.

~ Patricia Barnett

~*LAW FIVE*~

GATHER THE RIGHT TEAM
Select Your Support Structure and WINNING Team

Patricia Barnett

When I was a little girl my father would say, "Birds of a feather flock together." I had no idea what that meant at the time. Later I asked my father to explain it to me. He said, "That's easy, it means that people who are alike seem to group themselves together." He went on to say, "Patricia, remember this always, you will know a lot about a person by the company he or she keeps." Fast-forward several decades; while that particular saying is not as popular today, the truth of the saying remains. Simply put, like attracts like and this concept is especially powerful as it relates to The Law of 5's.

The Law of 5's states that we are the average of the sum total of the five people we associate with the most. Please note, I did not say the five people, who we like the most, or the five people we have the most fun with; instead, it is the five people with whom we spend the majority of our time. Few people identify and/or associate their results with those they surround themselves with most. Yet, once we become aware and understand this concept fully, it is evident that the Law of 5's has a powerful impact on our results and success or lack of it.

So you might be asking, "What does '*the average of the sum total*' really mean anyway and why is it important?" The best way to describe the Law of 5's and the power of it is: most likely the results of your life are usually not higher or lower than the average of those you are with most often. So if your goal is to earn $500,000 per year and everyone you spend time with is earning $100,000, it will be highly unlikely you will reach $500,000 until you begin associating most often with those who are earning what you desire. This applies whether you desire $100,000, $1,000,000 or $100,000,000.

Not only does this apply to money, it applies to health, relationships, attitude, discipline, activity, weight, drinking and almost everything else you can imagine.

So why is this? Let's take a deeper look.

Below are the results for two different groups of people:

Group A	**Group B**
Wealthy	Poor
Healthy	Sick
In Love	Out of Love
Positive	Negative
Happy	Miserable
Living Their Dreams	In Living Hell
Having FUN	Smoking/Drinking
Working Out	Overweight
Celebrating Results	Victim Stories

Even though these two groups look totally opposite, there is one thing that both groups have in common. Do you know what it is? You may be thinking it is the level of their activity and actions, which could be true, and yet it always begins with what they are tuned into with their thinking. It is the thinking and belief that creates the actions, creating the habits, that produce the results. Simply put, each group has a particular mindset.

Group A: The "wealthy group" has a wealthy mindset.

Group B: The "poor group" has a limited mindset.

Group A: The "healthy group" has a healthy mindset.

Group B: The "sick group" has a dis-eased mindset.

And so on.

Initially, it may look like it is the results of each group that are contagious. This is not the case at all; in fact, it is the *thinking, beliefs* and *mindset* that *are* contagious.

I remember introducing the Law of 5's to a new client one day and her reaction was priceless. She said that this concept sounded more like "profiling" and bordered on discrimination. I loved her reaction because it reminded me of my own reaction when my coach told me that I would never reach my next level of success until I surrounded myself with those more successful than I. He said, "Notice who you are asking for advice. Is it from people who are producing the results you would love or is it from those who have the results you currently have? Either way, you have a choice of who you will surround yourself with and the results you create long term."

Upon sharing this idea with my client, it became clear that she had been taking money advice from people who were broke, health advice from people who were sick and relationship advice from people in unhappy relationships. It wasn't long before she too saw the power of the Law of 5's and began changing her results by changing those with whom she associated with most.

On a side note, many times when people hear this concept for the first time, they think it has to do with only those people who are in the same room with them. The Law of 5's actually goes beyond whom you are working with or who is living in your home. It also includes the people on television, radio or Internet; anyone you are watching or listening to. The funny thing is that the marketing and promotions around a whole lot of programs has to do with "the drama" in life. As you watch, as you listen, simply be aware and ask yourself, "Is this in support of what I would love to create?" You might just be amazed at who you have been associating with most.

In creating wealth specifically, it is imperative to be aware of whom and what you surround yourself and also to ensure that you do surround yourself with a structure of support. Sometimes known as a Dream Team; we like to refer to it as your WINNING Team. Women especially, tend to buy into the "Lone Ranger" or "Super Hero" syndrome. Have you ever had one of these thoughts? "I'll just do it myself." or "If it's going to get done correctly, I've got to do it!" What we know for sure is that *everything* is easier with a team and quite frankly a whole lot more FUN!

A word of caution: BE AWARE OF THE CRABS!

THE POPULAR STORY OF THE CRAB BUCKET

One time a man was walking along the beach and saw another man fishing in the surf with a bait bucket beside him. As he drew closer, he saw that the bait bucket had no lid and had live crabs inside.

"Why don't you cover your bait bucket so the crabs won't escape?" he said.

"You don't understand," the man replied. "If there is one crab in the bucket it would surely crawl out very quickly. However, when there are many crabs in the bucket, if one tries to crawl up the side, the others grab hold of it and pull it back down so that it will share the same fate as the rest of them."

So it is with us. When one tries to do something different: get better grades, better jobs, improve themselves, escape their environment or dream big dreams, others people will try to drag that person back down into the "crab bucket" to share their same fate.

Moral of the story: know that crabs exist in your life. As you move forward, there will be those in your life who mean well and yet fear your moving ahead. Many times, these "crabs" show up as those closest to you – the well-meaning people who actually fear change themselves.

Recognize what's actually happening and continue to move forward in the direction of *your* goals and dreams!

My experience with the "crabs."

So here's the news: "Crabs" are everywhere. The great news is that you can have them in your life without them pulling you back into the "crab bucket" of life.

In looking back on my life, I have noticed that in creating new levels of health, wealth or love, "crabs" have accompanied me all along the way. Many times "crabs" can show up as the well-meaning people in our lives. Actually, those who show up "to pull you down" are simply a reflection of a hidden belief or fear within *us*.

Here is a great example to explain exactly what this means. In building my first business I was so excited to share my great vision and dreams with those in my inner circle. I had some people close to me say, "You don't have any business experience or even a college degree, how do you think you are going to succeed?" It was important for me to move forward even in the midst of this "reflective fear" if I was going to succeed.

As I grew, my business grew and so did my "inner circle." At this time I decided to grow my dreams and vision for a newly built and very large custom home. Thinking that I had moved away from the "crab bucket," I felt safe sharing my dream with a trusted colleague. What took me by surprise was her reaction of "How are *you* ever going to get a loan...especially in this market?" The sad part was it would be a couple of years later that the awareness came to me that I had allowed myself to buy into the belief of my new fellow "crab." It then dawned on me...crabs are everywhere. She didn't mean to "steal my dreams"; she was simply a mirror for my fears hidden within. Later I learned her reaction *also included her fears* of how she would be able get a loan in the state of the market.

The "crabs" can show up in business, with new relationships and even when we desire to change our state of health. With this awareness you will be more prepared to see the "crabs" when they show up and to understand that it is a terrific opportunity to continue forward, growing yourself and your dreams. You may be asking, "How do I do this?" Simply, steer clear of giving your attention to the "crabs"; instead, focus on surrounding yourself with a WINNING TEAM!

Below are 5 key areas for careful consideration and selection when building *your* WINNING team:

1. ***Mentor*** – An adviser or guide who has your same values and who has achieved the results you desire. This person can be someone you know personally or a "legend" you have never met. By studying the stories and roads to success, triumphs and setbacks, of those who have succeeded before you, your belief system begins to build. Mentors are great to emulate, especially in the beginning and when bumping up against obstacles and challenges. Remember this. If they did it...so can you!

2. ***Coach*** – Instructor and confidant that you meet with regularly who supports the expansion of your mindset, actions, growth and success while offering valuable feedback for creating results. This person is there to keep you on track and supports you in creating the appropriate mindset and taking the specific actions necessary to achieve your goals. Your coach guides you in the essential steps toward success, from beginning to end and every WIN along the way. *(This person also serves as a Mastermind Partner and/or Partner in Believing in the coaching process.)*

3. ***MasterMind*** – A group of like-minded thinkers heading along a similar pathway of success, as are you. These are

the people who are actively seeking their goals and who offer supportive ideas and experience to you. Participants in this group work together to create a greater "mind power." Where two or more are gathered with focused thought and intention, it is as if "magic" happens. Keep in mind that this is a trusted group and although you will gain much, your focus is to *give* in service to them as well.

4. ***Partner in Believing*** – A partner whom you meet with often who supports you in accountability and, when the road gets rocky, someone who believes in you even when you don't believe in yourself. It is important to know that you will be showing up as their partner in believing too. As you connect, remember, "All things are possible." Also, keep the time that you meet together to 15 to 20 minutes per week or a few minutes daily. Just be sure to stay within the agreed upon time frame.

   Caution: Sometimes, especially prior to creating the momentum and seeing the results you desire, there is a tendency to get "stuck" in the story of why things haven't happened. Stay tuned to the purpose and intention of the meeting. This is not the time to "fix" your partner. It is the time to stay tuned into the "Land of Solutions" coming from the mindset that "All things are possible." This is the time to celebrate the WINS and look for the "What's next?" in creating the vision. No "Pity Parties" allowed.

5. ***Team of Support*** – One or more people who work for and with you doing the tasks not in your area of expertise. This group leverages your time so that you can focus on being active in your zone of genius. Think of all the things others can do for you in your business and life that would

free you up to grow your business. Begin delegating to this team and then expand your team for full support in order to reach your goals quicker, faster and easier. This is the power of leverage.

On a side note - Leverage is power. The results of leverage are profound and exponential when used in your business. Even greater is to own a business based upon the power of leverage and in which the pay plan is also leveraged. One of the greatest business models that I know of personally, and have experienced rock star results first hand, is the business model of Network Marketing within the Direct Sales Industry. There is so much I have to share on this topic; the good, the bad, the ugly, what to do, what not to do and the incredible potential of living your dreams when you find the right fit with the perfect company for you. I have so much to share in fact; it is a whole other book within itself. For now, know that there is not only merit to the industry there is an opportunity where the sky is the limit for creating Wealth Mastery and I am living proof.

You may have heard it said, "Behind every great man, there is a great woman." *I believe that behind every really* **successful woman there is a WINNING Team!**

On every WINNING Team there is an MVP (most valuable player) and on your WINNING Team, the MVP is YOU! Because of this, it must be stressed that you become your own advocate. In speaking of the Law of 5's, *you* are the one person that you are with the most. Therefore, it is imperative you learn to be not only your own advocate but also your *best* advocate. This is what is known as "The Best Friend Practice." It is where you treat yourself just as you would your very best friend. You will not find anyone who has the potential to be a better friend to you than you. All you need to be a best friend is to know how to be a best friend.

Think about that for one moment. When you think of your best friend, what are the thoughts you think? When you speak with them, what do you say? When you are around them, what do you feel? A habit that many women have is to think critically of them selves. It is a pattern learned at an early age and sometimes we can be our very worst critics. One of the ways to re-pattern negative thoughts or fear thinking is first by noticing what we are saying to ourselves about ourselves. The key is to replace negative thoughts and feelings with positive thoughts, love, compassion and support. One of the ways to switch from negative to positive self-talk is by creating a mantra of success in support of your personal goals and dreams.

The reason it is so important to believe in yourself is you will never outperform your own self-image. Many people who have had great success don't only believe this; they know it to be true. One of the easiest ways to discover your inner beliefs about yourself is to look at your current results in life. Your results are reflective of your personal beliefs. Upon hearing this there may be a tendency to be critical or judgmental. It is in the awareness where the power to shift resides.

Another very powerful exercise in discovering your inner thoughts, identifying how you think about your self, and creating new patterns of being is an exercise introduced nearly thirty years ago by International Best Selling Author and one of the founders of the self-help movement, Louise Hay. In her book called *You Can Heal Your Life,* Ms. Hay shares the concept and the rewards of "Mirror Work." It is a very simple practice and at the same time incredibly powerful and immediately revealing.

It is one of my favorite exercises to share with my clients and one that I use personally. Simply go to your nearest mirror, look into your eyes and tell yourself what you see. Spend some time here to discover, uncover and recover your self-image. What is it that you see? This is a great opportunity to exercise your "Best Friend Practice." Can you look into your eyes...*really look into your own eyes*...and say, "I love you"? This might sound easy and the first response for many is, "Of course I can tell myself that I love myself." You may be surprised. For the fun of it, take a moment now to go to the nearest mirror and give your self some love. Remember; look into your own eyes, saying the words, "I love YOU!"

How was this for you? For first-timers, it is often and completely normal for emotions to come to the surface and sometimes, many tears to be shed. As babies, seeing our reflection in a mirror brings such joy and happiness. As we get older, we can become a bit more jaded, judgmental and even critical of our reflection. The essence of this experiment uncovers our self-worth, which at the end of the day our results in life reflect. The power of practicing this regularly over time is profound and transformative.

A Girl Named Amber

Once upon a time, in a land far, far away, there lived a young girl named Amber. This sweet, little girl was born just like all other children in the land: with a bright future, filled with magnificent potential and extraordinary possibilities as well as the guarantee for obstacles to face and challenges to overcome.

Amber's challenges began just shortly after arriving home from the hospital after birth. Although she was born to a family that truly did love her - this family was living a legacy of a horrible spell cast upon it generations before. The spell was that life would be incredibly hard – an existence of heartbreaking dysfunction, dis-ease and a lifetime of abuse and addiction to run rampant in their castle.

From the very beginning, Amber's life was filled with chaos, volatility, immense fear and deep despair. A mother who came from a long line of witches and warlocks, a step-sister who had been exposed to a life of evil, and a father doing his very best to protect his family from ogres and villains while battling a curse of his own inner demons, Amber longed for a life of beauty, security, joy, fun and above all...Love.

By the time Amber was five years old, it was as if Amber had lived well beyond a lifetime of hurt, sadness, pain and sorrow. She had heard of the great success of Cinderella and even in the midst of her darkest days, Amber kept the dream alive that one day she too would be free. And one day, Amber's dream came true. Suddenly one night, she was sent to live with a different King and Queen in a new land, far, far away.

With such a sudden shift in circumstances and dramatic journey to the new land, upon arriving Amber was actually in even deeper despair: weak, meek, and scared of her own shadow. As if the "spirit of life" had left her little soul, Amber would rarely smile or make eye contact with others and would hide from her own reflection. After settling in to her new room and becoming familiar with new her surroundings, the queen invited Amber for afternoon tea.

"*Sweetest Amber,*" *the queen began, "My name is Queen Abigail Patrinia. It's a long name for a young girl like you to remember. Please feel free to call me 'AP'." Amber immediately felt love and trust for the queen. "The question I have for you, young Amber, is this." The queen continued, "What is your greatest wish?" In an instant Amber realized that it was as if AP seemed to be more of a real life "Fairy God Mother" rather than a queen.*

Amber felt a stir of hope and shared her dream with the queen, "I want to be happy, healthy, beautiful and most of all I want to feel truly loved." AP replied, "Your wish is my command, sweetest Amber; but first you must know this, to be loved by others, you must first love yourself. When you do, true love will follow along with happiness, health and beauty on the inside of you as well as on the outside. In fact everywhere your eyes can see you will find all things beautiful and lovely. We will begin with the transformation first thing in the morning."

Amber awakened early the next morning with a renewed hope and enthusiasm, ready to step into her new, lovely and beautiful life. Amber searched the palace for AP and found her in a beautiful room sitting next to a magnificent mirror. As Amber entered the room, AP was filled with such joy to introduce Amber to the "Magic Mirror." Gently leading the sweet young girl to the mirror, AP said, "Amber, this is called your 'Magic Mirror.' It is an incredibly powerful tool, much like having your very own magic wand. Used correctly, you will certainly see beautiful and magnificent results. The rules for correct application are very simple." AP continued, " Look at yourself in the mirror. Look into your own eyes and say out loud, 'I love myself'."

Amber was so excited. "That's easy," she exclaimed! As she raced to the mirror, Amber found her own gaze and looking deeply into her own eyes, tears began to form and rolled down her face like a small river. With a look of disgust, Amber quickly turned away and yelled, "I can't do this AP! All I see in that mirror is an ugly, unlovable girl. Your mirror must be broken because I do not love her at all."

AP knew that even though this exercise was simple, it did not always mean that it would be easy. Each day the king and the queen would take Amber to the 'magic mirror.' Each day the king would speak to the young Amber as if he were singing an enchanting song to her, "Amber, can you see the most beautiful, lovely, wonderful girl that we see?" Each day Amber would do her best to see the beauty in the reflection of herself looking back. At first it began with a whisper, "I love myself," and with that love, the little girl in the mirror smiled back.

Day by day, getting stronger in every way, over time the transformation became evident. Soon Amber was running to the 'magic mirror', smiling, dancing, waving her hands in the air, singing and shouting from the top of her lungs, "I love myself. I Love Myself. I Love My Self!"

Not only was there a new shift in meeting with the "magic mirror," Amber's results in life reflected the mirror work. She began to exude beauty from deep within. As her self-image grew, her confidence soared and it showed in all areas of her life. Right before her very eyes, Amber transformed into a royal princess. She exuded beauty from the inside out and was filled with passion, enthusiasm and love for her life.

Princess Amber became her own best friend. Life became fun and soon she became great friends with the other princesses in the land. Smiling, laughing, dreaming, playing and skipping through her new life, Amber had an awareness the she was finally living her dreams; that she was finally free.

Upon realizing that her deepest desires had come true: a life of love, health, happiness and freedom, Amber ran to AP in celebration and said, "I did it AP! I am living my dreams, my wish has come true!" Queen Abigail Patrinia replied back, "Princess Amber, you have tapped into the very thing that makes the world go around. Love. Love for the Life you have been given and Love for Life itself."

Truly, Amber had found her very own magic wand and one of the most powerful keys to living happily ever after.

So, what are the thoughts that come to mind after reading *The Story of Amber?*

- *Cute story?*

- *Could it really be that simple?*

- *Is it possible that the "magic mirror" really exists?*

- *Could the "magic mirror" work for me?*

The answer, a resounding YES!

One of the "objections" that comes up upon the introduction of this exercise is the belief, many times deeply hidden belief, that to love our selves is somehow a sin. I think many of our ancestors misread or misinterpreted the original memo sent out about this topic. Is it possible that there has been confusion in the love "of" self versus the love "for" self?

Our life itself is one of the greatest gifts we have ever been given. Along with life, we have been given additional gifts and talents to be used in making this world a better place. We know that when we appreciate or give love to *anything* it is the equivalent of our very own "miracle-grow." For some reason we have a culture today of women comparing, judging, and many times not willing to even see the beauty or the love that resides within each and every one of us. Many times we as women, look outside of ourselves for validation, appreciation, and love. Appreciate, love and become your very own best friend. This is the beginning of allowing love and appreciation from other people and receiving the good you are truly worth.

As stated in the story, it is a simple exercise and yet it is a process. I know the power of the process and have seen the extraordinary results of this practice first hand, over and over and over. Although the story of *A Girl Named Amber* is simply a story, the most profound results I have ever witnessed firsthand was with my darling niece named Amber who came to live with my husband and me for a summer when she was five years old. We used the "magic mirror" and the results were exceptional and literally life changing in a very short period of time.

Eventually Amber came to live with us full time and in the brilliant metamorphosis of her life, transformed from our darling niece into our "beautiful, lovely and wonderful" daughter. Over time, there were many "tools" that Amber worked with to transform and create the life she loves living. Looking back, she says that the "magic mirror" is one of the most powerful in her repertoire for self-development and achieving results.

Today, Amber is a highly skilled and successful makeup artist working in West Hollywood, CA. She is an absolute and true beauty on the inside *and* on the outside. Amber is a confident professional who thrives in one of the largest cities and competitive industries. She continues to dream and continues to live her dreams: a healthy life of fulfillment, happiness and love...truly living happily ever after.

Write Your Self a Love Letter

As stated earlier, affirmations are a powerful tool in being your own best friend. This is a way to show yourself some love and give a boost to your self-esteem in the process. Your affirmations could be similar to a mantra and could also be things that you like about yourself, words of inspiration and encouragement as well as anything that will lift your spirits and lift you up for the day ahead. Think of this as writing a little love note of five affirmations and/or appreciations to yourself each day. With consistent action, you will soon see profound results.

Sample Mantra:

"Every day and in every way, I am getting better and better."

"Every day and in every way, I am creating increased wealth."

"Every day and in every way, I am loving my life."

"Every day and in every way, I am creating my dreams."

Sample Inspiration:

"I believe in YOU!"

"Today is a great day to be your best!"

"You were made for greatness."

"Today take action and moving closer to my goal."

"You can do it!"

As you empower yourself, you become your very own cheerleader versus your worst enemy. In creating a greater self-image, you literally change those who are attracted *to you* and collapse the time it takes to reach your goals. By increasing the belief in yourself, you increase your results.

As a result of surrounding yourself with a WINNING Team and becoming the MVP of your team, you will BE unstoppable.

LAW FIVE - ACTION STEPS

GATHER THE RIGHT TEAM

Select Your Support Structure and Winning Team

Action Steps:

1. Select your WINNING Team – Carefully choose your support structure (mentor, coach, mastermind group and partners in believing).

2. Create your Team of Support – Choose people with the qualities below:

   • They are aligned with your core values and believe in you and your mission.
   • They have excellent skills and experience. (Look for the people who have the skills that you don't.)
   • They are teachable people who have a true desire to help others.
   • They are honest, focused and work cheerfully and diligently.
   • They are flexible, creative and FUN.

3. Become your own advocate – Use *your* "Magic Mirror" regularly. Also, write five affirmations daily that empower you. Then "put them on" and take them with you through your day.

Our dreams are like lovers...

If you pay attention, court them, invite them, be kind and loving to them, and invest thought, time and resources in them, your dreams will become real.

~ Lynn Kitchen

~*LAW SIX*~

CREATE A BLUEPRINT FOR SUCCESS

Build Business, Strategic and Tactical Plans

Lynn Kitchen

All things emanate from VISION. WHAT are you creating? Where are you going?

Your business is the VEHICLE for your LIFE – the consciousness by which you construct the structures that will carry your business forward. Imagine the car you drive taking you places, and into which you strap your precious babies in the back seat. In the same way, your business is carrying you and all your loved ones forward into all-your-dreams-come-true land!

Put your VEHICLE on WHEELS with our model to help you move forward more quickly! This WHEEL Business Blueprint is a clear and elegant structure. It is designed for the beginner, but it can be expanded in scope for the more mature enterprise. The important thing is to understand how it all fits together and take the time to make it uniquely YOURS.

Think of it as a board game, with a starting point on the left, with your game piece moving clockwise around the wheel, back to the beginning. Arranged like spokes in the wheel, the top half of the wheel is called YOUR STRATEGIC PLAN, which is structuring and working ON your business. The bottom half of the wheel is called YOUR TACTICAL PLAN, which is structuring and working IN your business.

Before you begin, be sure you have already created your company's LEGAL framework – whether a single proprietorship, a limited liability corporation, a C corporation, etc. Also be sure to have next to you the "3 Year Vision Statement" that you have written. This will help guide you, because it is a written PLAN for your Business Life!

Now, please draw the Wheel, and you can fill in the pie sections as we go.

Action Steps Part 1 - Business Plan

1. Decide the legal structure – get legal help if needed.
2. Write a 3-Year Vision Statement – Your Leadership Plan for Your Business Life.
3. Draw the "Wheel" – A Blueprint of your Business.

Now you are ready to fill in the sections of your wheel!

THE WHEEL GOES ROUND – from top to bottom and round and round!

WHEEL OF BUSINESS SUCCESS

Your wheel is divided into six segments, or spokes. Notice there are the top 3 that are related, and the bottom 3 are related. Your business can be described in two halves, Strategic and Tactical. These are words that you can associate readily with "Strategy" and "Action" – it's the two halves of any endeavor, like yin and yang, or like the two halves of a walnut inside the casing. There is an interplay between the halves, yet you must have both to operate smoothly.

Think of it this way: those hours you spend working ON your business – that is Strategic Planning - the top 3 segments. It encompasses planning out the marketing, financing and managing the various parts of your business. These 3 are considered "Disciplines" of business. These disciplines undergird and support the production end of the business.

Now think of those hours you spend working IN your business – that is Tactical Planning – the bottom 3 segments. It encompasses actions you take – finding your clients, engaging them into becoming clients, and finally delivering the services for which they will pay you. These 3 are the "Activities" of your business that become the crucial point of sale upon which the whole wheel torques forward!

So let's try them on here:

Action Steps Part 2 – Fill Out Your Segments for Strategic Plan – segments 1,2, and 3.

These are the "Disciplines," the support FOR the business.

Spoke #1 – Marketing Plan – Answer these questions:

1) Who are my clients?
2) Where do I find them?
3) Why do they buy?

(Write and develop an overall marketing plan.)

Spoke #2 – Financial Plan – Put these systems in place:

1) Set up a Business Checking Account (MUST be separate from personal).
2) Create a Budget – You need a Start-up Budget, a 1-Year Budget broken down into 12 months. This helps you manage your expectations as well as your money! KNOW what your business will require in advance!
3) Build Accounting Systems – Get help on this. This is for tracking all your sales and expenses so you can create financial reports and stay accountable!

Spoke #3 – Management Plan – Write a paragraph about what you will NEED to support the business and keep it operational and then what you will need to GROW.

1) Systems
2) People
3) Product Production or New Product Expansion

STARTING POINT – The two halves go together in sequence. You begin with your marketing plan. Write it out. Next, you work on your financial underpinnings – this will get you "set up." Third, you ask what systems, people or products you will need to have in place. See, you are halfway around the WHEEL!

Now you are ready for the fun part, where the real action is – your clients!

Action Steps Part 3 – Fill Out the Segments for Tactical Plan – Segments 4, 5 and 6. These are the "Activities," the daily actions of your business.

Spoke #4 – Attracting Clients – Your Client "Funnel"

1) What is your funnel? Describe it.
2) How do you attract clients and fill the funnel?
3) Referrals – Are you asking for referrals all the time?

Spoke # 5 – Client Enrollment

1) Approach – How do you initiate conversation?
2) Connect – List the effective ways you connect and engage.
3) Serve, not Sell – Write about how it makes you feel to serve your clients.

Spoke #6 – Delivery of Goods/Service

1) Signup, registration and/or invoicing.
2) Collect payment.
3) Deliver and surprise!

Congratulations! You have successfully outlined your plans for the STRATEGIC half of your business and for the TACTICAL half of your business.

You can see how you START with marketing, move to finance, move to management. With these three areas in order you can progress to segment 4.

There you plan how you will get your clients. You progress to what you will say to them once you find them, and finally how you will sign them up, collect the money and deliver your goods or services.

Guess what! One turn of the wheel deserves another! Once you have made your first sales, then you go around the wheel again! You check your marketing strategy, you tally your sales and watch your wallet, you check your management needs. Then you go out and see more clients!

The wheel becomes easier over time. It's designed to be easy and elegant. As your sales grow, you will adjust your needs in all the six segments. The cool thing is that at any point, if something is not working in your business, by having this WHEEL MODEL, you can more quickly identify where the clog is happening. For example, what if you are a single entrepreneur wearing all the hats? At a certain point in sales, in order to function and sustain any further growth, you will need to concentrate on segment #3 – determine if it's time to add more people to support you, or a new software system.

This is a clear way to see your business from an ORGANIC point of view, seeing all the parts working together as a whole. You can calendar your week, giving one day a week to working ON your business, and four days to working IN your business, for example. You will clearly know which hat you are wearing at what day of the week! You will be a better businesswoman and a happier, more productive owner. And you can do what you have been put on this planet to do – give your unique gifts and talents to the world by means of YOU!

WHEE! ENJOY the WHEEL. Feel the increased logic and freedom it allows you. It's your Blueprint For Success!

LAW SIX - ACTION STEPS

CREATE A BLUEPRINT FOR SUCCESS

Build Business, Strategic and Tactical Plans

Action Steps:

1. Create your 3-year vision statement specifically for your business – see yourself as the entrepreneur you want to be in 3 years time.

2. Draw your "WHEEL" in a dedicated notebook – it's a simple, elegant blueprint for your business that prioritizes your actions into sequential sections.

3. Complete each section of your wheel, 1 through 6, and notice how it gives you clarity as you focus on one section and then move to the next, just like a board game. It is repeatable. Each round brings you greater clarity, focus and purpose. If you need help, be sure to contact me!

Make time to tap into the Source within you. When you do, you will find a reservoir of full potential to support you in all of your endeavors.

~ Julie Jones Hamilton

~*LAW SEVEN*~

DEVELOP SYSTEMS THAT WORK

Create Replicable Processes and Methods

Julie Jones Hamilton

"Management works in the system; leadership works on the system."

~Steven R. Covey

We, as women, know that we perform our best when we operate within a structure. In today's world many women carry on a family, a business and philanthropy combined.

For me to be a success in all of my affairs, I rely upon a system I discovered on my journey twenty-two years ago in substance recovery. Every day I apply life giving principles and specific structures to create the life I love living. After all these years how did I do it? I did it with systems that work, one step at a time. When you are true to your systems, your systems are true to you!

When we develop systems that work in our business and life, we find they are easily to replicate. As children, many of us went to school in a structured system. We may have come home to homework, group activities or chores and responsibilities. No matter what our schedule might have been we were operating within a system. As we matured into women: as leaders, wives, students, professionals, business owners or mothers, we realized life is more manageable when we develop systems. So, how do we do this?

When building a successful business and life we love, we wear many different "hats" at any given moment. As a woman in business we may wear three hats, *Technician, Manager and Entrepreneur.*

It is imperative that we understand the difference between each hat so that each system runs smoothly and effectively. When each hat is defined as the *Technician, Manager or Entrepreneur,* then all situations can be designated to the proper place.

Let's have a closer look at the systems involved within each of the three hats a business owner may wear.

Hat #1, "The Technician"
The Technician is usually the *doer* who implements the structures and creates the system. The systems lay the foundation for consistency in a smooth-running company. In the home the Technician may be the one who works on the activities, the organization or a social calendar schedule.

As a business owner, when programs need writing and products need to be made and sold, the Technician is the one who initiates the creative strategies.

The Technician may use others, an assistant, a team or partner who is supportive in collaborative ways with other activities.

It is the Technician's responsibility to be able to portray a clear, concise, detailed vision of the direction in which the company is moving. Here are some additional questions to ask when uncovering your objectives.

- What is your primary purpose for your business?
- What does your business provide?
- What is the biggest problem you solve for your customers?
- Who does your business serve and what are the benefits of your services?
- What are the best practices in your business?

After answering these questions, your decision-making process will be more efficient. However, it is also very important to know your "Why?" Because, it will sustain the momentum when you are in the process of building your business, especially when conditions may appear to be less than perfect. We all have bumps and valleys and our "Why" allows us to stay focused on our end results. What is your "Why"? Why are you in business? What is your primary purpose of being a business owner? Is it to do something you're skilled at, believe in or love? Is it to create the flexibility so you could do what you want when you want? Is it to spend more time with your family, friends or loved ones? Is it your goal to be the best in your industry?

In knowing your "Why," when times seem challenging your "Why" will strengthen your resolve to continue moving forward.

Hat #2, "The Manager"

The Manager oversees and makes the decisions for the most effective services, best business practices, best products to offer and management of the employees in a business. The Manager oversees the efficiency of the business, ensuring that all runs smoothly. The Manager may oversee the account receivables and payables, maintenance and other activities. She plans timeframes, scheduling, and creates connections. She communicates with employees, leads team members and oversees the business goals, checklists and customer relationships. In business, the Manager may also assist in navigating the direction of the company.

The Manager ensures that all of the goals are in alignment with the mission and business plan and that all of the systems are in alignment with the vision.

What are some of the responsibilities of a manager?

Traditionally, the Manager's description and responsibilities include the following:

- *Plans:* planning the operation and function of the family and business. A business manager is assigned responsibility in a way that accomplishes the goals for which she is responsible.
- *Organizes and Implements*: organizing the production of work; the workforce, members and training if necessary in a way that accomplishes the desired and required outcomes to meet the goals.
- *Directs:* provides the employees resources and enough guidance, direction, leadership and support necessary to ensure success.

- *Monitors*: follows up in achieving the goals and checks to see they are being carried out in such a way that its accomplishment is assured.
- *Evaluates*: reviews and assesses the success of the goal and the allocation of employees and resources.

A lack of clear performance expectations is cited as *the* contributing factor for happiness or unhappiness in life and in a business. Being very specific and communicating expectation, responsibilities and job descriptions is essential as a manager. When defined, they affect a sense of participation in a venture larger than oneself and the feelings of engagement, motivation, and teamwork for everyone involved.

Hat #3, "The Entrepreneur"

The Entrepreneur in a business is the dreamer, the inventor and the visionary of the company. She sees the big picture, the possibilities of accomplishment and the direction in which the vision grows. An entrepreneur makes and encourages others to make the necessary steps in discovering ways in achieving the results. She organizes and operates a business or enterprise, usually with considerable initiative and risk.

A true entrepreneurial essence is to: define, invest, build and repeat, knowing you need to be both a leader and a manager in that order. She always starts as a leader and then, as she grows, finds a manager. In running a smooth life and business a woman would benefit by looking closely at what is involved in being an entrepreneur.

WOMEN IN BUSINESS

In today's world it is undoubtedly the best time for female entrepreneurs. According to research from American Express OPEN Forum, women are starting an average of 1,200 businesses a day – up from 740 a day the year prior. The growth of women-owned firms continues to outpace the national average, plus they now lead growth in eight of the top thirteen industries in America and are paving the way for women globally.

Discover in the next three questions if you are an entrepreneur.

Are You Approachable?

A good exercise in being approachable and in building team camaraderie with sound leadership is to encourage activities outside the workplace. It is also a great way to empower team members and provide them with a sense of purpose other than only focusing on the company's bottom line.

Creating a Climate of Increase?

In smaller businesses, staying focused on the mission of the company and who it services, along with core values and customer and employee service, will create a sense of security and increase that comes with knowing that everyone is building a foundation on solid ground.

Do you lead by example?

A leader leads by example and is reliable, credible and cares about herself and others. Are you *being* a woman who is an entrepreneur? When it comes to a leader's work performance, do you hold yourself to a higher standard – one your team wants to emulate? Be a woman of increase. If your clients and employees see you being professional, going the extra mile and caring about the work in the way you want them to, then you bet they will want to do the same.

Working *ON* Your Business

Working **ON** your business is production and creation. It is mapping out your systems to be accessible and repeatable. It's the time you spend setting up your initial processes and developments. It could be the writing of a program, workshop or teaching tools, or it could be the book, manual or services you provide. Usually once this process is complete it is unnecessary to create it again, unless you are creating updates and add-ons.

Working *IN* Your Business

Recognize that business is generated through relationships and action. While working **IN** your business, the more you are in front of others, the more you are able to serve your clients and give exposure to your business.

The more you engage in action, the more support you will discover for your business and goals. The more support you discover for your business and goals, the closer you become in creating Wealth Mastery. This all works within a system.

Create a Time Study

Tracking the time you spend and deciding where the best value lies are the keys in achieving success. A "Time Study" assists you in becoming proficient in your daily actions. In switching "hats" and organizing your time and resources, consider the following questions.

- How much time do I spend on creating product or content?

- What is the amount of time I spend in creating my business daily, weekly, monthly?

- Am I creating my work for repeatable production?

- Do I put my efforts in service or creating?

- Do I create blocks of time to get things done?

- Do I work on one project until it is completed?

- Do I work on many things at the same time?

- Do I have timelines for finishing projects?

- Are my workspace and projects organized?

- How much time and investment do I spend on networking, phone calls or client calls?

- Do I hold myself accountable as a leader for my team and myself?

- Am I serious about my success?

Wherever you place your focus, will then begin to expand. Be mindful if you place your focus upon something that takes you away from the production of your daily business, then you will need a system to identify where you spend your most valuable resource... your time.

Systems such as products creation, logos, branding, websites, content, ... are simple and can be created with effective tools and support in a digital global market. Today, we can easily create our own websites or find others who will do the work for us quickly and affordably.

There are a myriad of applications once you have developed systems that work. Other systems such as timelines, products, projections, release dates, etc., are activities that are easily scheduled in a timely manner with effective collaborative online software such as Asana and Google Drive. Implementing systems allows the work with others to be easily replicated and duplicated.

Being a successful business owner or entrepreneur is about being creative and confident with ease and grace. The more you see your tasks as a structured pattern of systems, the easier it becomes to deliver your gifts, talents and love to the world one step at a time.

Here are action steps that assist you in gaining clarity in developing systems that will work for you.

Action Step #1 – ARE YOU WORKING *ON* OR WORKING *IN* YOUR BUSINESS?

In being a business owner or entrepreneur, it is critical to identify if you are *working ON* your business or *working IN* your business.

As mentioned in LAW SIX, working **ON** your business is *"YOUR STRATEGIC PLAN."* It is the systems needed in marketing, management, production and financing. It is also creating the consistent and simple implementation of allowing your systems to be replicable and repeatable.

Working *IN* your business is being a leader and creating *"YOUR TACTICAL PLAN."* It is generating, through relationships and action, the exposure needed for yourself and your business. It is giving excellent service and being a woman of increase.

To discover if you are working *ON* your business or *IN* your business, ask yourself the following questions:

- Do I gauge or keep track of time in all areas of my business?

- What are the responsibilities and the decisions I spend my time on making?

- Do I spend time devoted to developing products, making calls or on inventory, paperwork and billing, etc.?

- What are the projects or tasks I dread to do?

- Do I reach out and make contact with others in my industry, and if so, how often and when?

- What is the amount of time I devote to cultivating clients and relationships?

- Do I belong to any networking groups or clubs?

- Do I interact with others on a daily, weekly, monthly basis?

- What are the ways I generate resources?

- How much time do I spend working on my business in a week, a month or a year?

- Do I invest time and resources in my own personal growth and knowledge?

Look over your answers and begin to understand how they fit within your systems. Look for the different patterns in which you spend time working *ON* your business or *IN* your business.

Your answers share with you insights into your areas of priorities, strengths and weaknesses. Notice if this insight aligns with your core values. Then ask the question, "In what areas would I add more to or subtract from?"

Action Step #2 – Create a Time Inventory

Applying the answers from the Time Study, we now look at another time technique called the "Time Inventory." It is created for you to see the benefits of what and where you spend most of your valuable time.

To begin, take a look at the projects only you could do to maximize your energy and potential; it will probably be in the area of your own expertise. Make a list of your expertise and a list of the activities only you can do, and then make a list of the activities you would delegate to others.

This list will change as you grow with your business and with your staff; however, starting out in business, many of us do everything at first. It is during this time you need to be conscientious of where you place your focus, time and energy.

- Do you have daily or weekly business meetings or consulting calls?

- How much time does each call take?

- Do you have daily, weekly or monthly preparations to perform in order for your office to run smoothly?

- How much time does it take you to perform your duties, create your product or sell your product?

- How much time are you spending working *ON* your business?

- How much time do you spend working *IN* your business?

- Do you study, have trainings or educational meetings? If so, how much time do you devote to each?

Track your time and then decide where is the best value for you to place your focus to accomplish your goals?

Again, this information gives you insight. When I applied this technique I was surprised to see how many hours I spent on the small tasks one of my team members loves to do. I also noticed I spent too much time searching for things when I was shown an easier and quicker way.

Because I created a "Time Inventory" I am able to use this valuable system, which allows me time to concentrate on the work I love that only I can do.

Action Step #3 – Calendar-ize

- Create a calendar with a daily schedule of your time spent working *ON* or *IN* your business.

Creating a calendar allows you an overview to a smooth and efficient workweek. Creating a schedule of your tasks enables the most effective use of your time, talent and resources. We all know that time efficiency in any business creates success.

- Calendar-ize all your daily activities onto a schedule.

Calendar-izing your daily activity supports you in being disciplined, on time and efficient in your life and business. It is a valuable resource to use. Having my daily activities on a calendar allows me to plan my weekly, monthly and yearly schedule. It offers me confidence in the work I do and allows me to stay focused and organized.

By all means, remember to schedule a day or two a week for rest and fun. Yes, calendar-ize that into your schedule, too! Wealth Mastery is obtained when we come from being in harmony with a nourished life in *all* areas.

LAW SEVEN - ACTION STEPS

DEVELOP SYSTEMS THAT WORK

Create Replicable Processes and Methods

Action Steps:

1. Determine if you are working *ON* or *IN* your business.

2. Create a Time Inventory.

3. Calendar-ize all your daily activities onto a schedule.

Abundance is ever-present.

It is a state of mind.

~ Lynn Kitchen

~*LAW EIGHT*~

FINANCE YOUR DREAM
Apply the Best Options and Resources Available

Lynn Kitchen

"Your dreams are closer than you think."

– Prince Ojong, *The Miraculous Millionaire: A Sensible Approach To Financial Freedom*

Our dreams are like lovers...if you pay attention, court them, invite them, be kind and loving to them, and discover all you can about them, you will find out they will reveal to you all the various likes and dislikes – this is information that will make the relationship WORK! Your dream is the same. You must invest thought, time and resources to make your dream a reality.

So many dreams are quashed because the dreamer says, "I can't – I don't have the money." If that's you, then know you are killing the deal before you begin! It may be true you don't have the OBVIOUS financial means easily accessible at this moment. However, it is imperative to understand that...you do have the means!

There are multiple options and resources that are available to you – if you are open to doing some research, doing some high-possibility list making and taking some bold actions! By means of thinking newly and taking action, you can create a possibility where before there appeared to be none.

Everyone Can Finance Her Dream!

I have worked for years with people who have a dream and they want to know the best way to finance it. As a professional money manager for over thirty-five years, I counseled individuals, couples, entrepreneurs, companies and non-profits how to buy houses, send children to college, open businesses, go on luxury vacations, build for retirement, buy second homes, buy out a competitor's business, send grandchildren to college, create legacies, build buildings and corporations. The list goes on and on.

I have also worked with young people, just beginning, who had very little except hope and energy. They were willing to learn, and to make the sacrifices that it may take to forego spending money on a personal indulgence in order to build resources that could finance their future choices in life.

Whatever your situation, whether you have assets you can use to finance your dream or whether you do not, there is one way to begin: Create a possibilities checklist! I call it a Source List.

WHAT NOT TO DO...BEG, BORROW OR STEAL!
(Well, borrowing might work, but groveling or stealing is definitely not in your best interest!)
WHAT TO DO – WRITE a "Source List."

ACTION STEP: Create a Source List and a Vision Statement

A source list is a possibilities list. The idea is to list as many possible sources that you can think of – at least 10 – then take a break, come back and write down 10 more! Yes, the goal is 20! You have more sources than you know. Everyone does!

A source list can also be, in itself, a "dream list." That's right...dream up some cool sources that you would love! Let your imagination really be free here. What if...!

One young entrepreneur, Sally, with whom I worked, took an extra step of creating a written vision for the ultimate Source she wanted, writing in the present tense as if she already was gratefully in receipt of the funding. She then read that vision statement to herself twice a day, visualizing receiving the check from her perfect Source Funder.

Here is Sally's vision statement: "I am so happy and grateful now that I have received a 5-year note of $50,000 at 2% interest from a female angel investor who believes in me, in my project, in my potential, and who is introducing me to 3 new customers whose orders are now doubling my business."

Within one month, Sally met a woman at a networking event who loaned her the exact amount and brought her not three, but five new referral clients who virtually guaranteed the payback of the loan in less than two years!

This positive vision statement created the precise mindset necessary to attract the exact right condition and resource Sally desired. You can do this too!

Your Source List

"If you don't create a good message about your dreams, those who were created to pay for it can't find it. Speak them out and you will find those God created to finance it."

– Israelmore Ayivor

When you read the above quote, I hope that what jumps out at you are these words..."those who were created to pay for (your dream)".... Yes, the Source Exists! You get to find it!

Let's get started.

SELF-FUNDING – If you already have assets, it becomes a choice, a weighing of which asset makes the wisest choice relative to other assets. Examples:

Liquid Assets – Savings – do you have savings or CDs to invest in your dream?

Liquid Assets – Investments – do you own stocks, bonds or mutual funds you can readily cash out?
Collectibles – do you own artwork, furniture, jewelry or other valuables to sell?

Illiquid Assets – do you have property, homes, annuities or insurance policies you own that can be borrowed against? Refinance?

CAUTION – I do not recommend cashing in your retirement assets, although you will hear many people loosely advise, "Hey, just liquidate your IRA or your 401K – you've saved it for yourself." Not wise. That money represents tax-deferred savings you put away from earlier good earning years. I have seen many people wipe out their retirement, risk it all on a business that didn't do well, and then they were doubly penalized. Explore all other avenues first – you will find a source that's better!

Income – Your own income is a source! In the case that you have a job and you are looking to fund your dream (which is secondary):

a) You can save more of what you earn to fund your dream. (Spend less to finance your future dream.)

b) Personal Loans – You can borrow money from friends, family or others with a promissory note to pay the loan back from your current income (allowing all money earned in your new dream business to be reinvested properly in the business).

BORROWING – Using future income from your business, business loans can be researched. Traditional loans, equipment or receivables financing is available at banks, community banks, credit unions or small business agencies (SBA loans). Check out www.SBA.gov. There may be some specialty categories that apply to you.

In most cases, traditional bank loans are very difficult to obtain unless you already have a great deal of financial wealth, and even then, you may be required to sign a personal obligatory note that holds you personally responsible for the loan of the business.

Create a PRIVATE FINANCIER GROUP – You can make a list of people who might make a small loan each, gathering all loans into a PFG – Private Finance Group – for which you construct a payback schedule, a little to each person each month. For example, if you need to raise $50,000 to start your business, find 5 people willing to loan you $10,000 each; 10 people willing to loan $5000 each; or 20 people willing to loan $2500 each. You get the picture.

Create a low-end CROWDFUNDING campaign – for smaller amounts of money there are many social media sites now that allow enterprising people to create a campaign and ask for even smaller amounts of money from their lists of hundreds of friends or those on their email list. One example is www.YouFundMe.com. Others are www.Kickstarter.com and www.Indiegogo.com.

MEET-UP GROUPS – yes, that's right! You can meet other entrepreneurs and funders in meet-up groups that specialize in just that! A great example can be found at TechCocktail, a lively group that meets in major cities like Chicago, Washington, DC, and Las Vegas, and growing! Check out http://women2.com/ and http://tech.co/events/.

Find a MICRO-FUNDER – new sources of money for start-up businesses are popping up in the marketplace. Micro-funding is when a group of investors or non-profits lend small amounts of start-up funds and arrange payback. Available primarily in third world countries, women can often borrow as little as $100 or $500 and pay it back weekly to get a small, home-based business going. I believe more will be made available for US-based women-owned businesses in the near future. Even SBA has a micro-lending division now: www.SBA.gov.

GRANTS – go to www.FederalGrants.com. There are grants for businesses that qualify within certain industries or parameters set up by the federal government. There are grants from the National Science Foundation, for example, for companies in the science or tech space.

http://www.forbes.com/sites/drewhendricks/2013/10/31/4-great-tips-for-finding-funding-for-your-startup.

Sophisticated FINANCING

Business owners with a strong track record and assets can find financing in sophisticated financial arenas such as venture capital, angel investors and private placements.

ANGEL GROUPS & VENTURE CAPITAL GROUPS – You have seen the popular show *SharkTank*, where entrepreneurs pitch their new business ideas to a panel of investors hoping to gain a financial partnership arrangement. This is a real-world phenomenon....not just on TV. But it is just as rigorous. You will need to be prepared with solid financials, business plans and some incentives for investors to risk their capital in your venture. Also know that those investors give you much needed start-up capital, but they require you to give them a high percentage ownership of your company.

There are new financial support groups for women popping up everywhere both in the US, Canada, Europe and elsewhere. Investor groups willing to make private loans or grants (like an angel) are worth researching (see article below). This is especially true in the "tech" or "medical" fields.

Try searching on Google for local and regional angel investor groups. And don't forget to research your local city and county for developmental agency funds where counties are trying to incentivize more jobs in their area. For example, look for "Business Incubators."

Of course venture capital firms abound, especially in Silicon Valley, like 500 Start-ups, or hundreds more, some specializing in seed funds and accelerator, early stage funding.

http://tech.co/exxclaim-capital-vc-fund-womens-health-2014-07

http://tech.co/femanomics-105-women-in-venture-capital-and-angel-investment-2012-05

http://www.inc.com/jill-krasny/5-documentaries-to-watch-this-spring.html

PRIVATE PLACEMENTS – the Securities Industry sets forth a way for small to medium-sized companies to raise money from a group of potential investors. A portion of the company is "sold" to an investor group of sophisticated, accredited investors at a pre-arranged price, with a specified holding period, creating a private "market" for the shares.

PUBLIC UNDERWRITINGS – the Securities Industry provides a method for companies that meet specified financial metrics to become publicly listed, creating a continuous public market for their shares. Large major financial firms pool together funds to create a syndicate to support the initial pricing and offering of the shares to the public.

The important thing is to begin – create your source list. You may not know yet the source of the funds that will eventually fund your dreams. Just know that the Source Exists!!

LAW EIGHT - ACTION STEPS

FINANCE YOUR DREAM

Apply the Best Options and Resources Available

Action Steps:

1. Commit to finding the source of your funding! Determine the foundational expenses, budget and all cash flow projections for your business. Get crystal clear about your needs.

2. Self-funding: list your current assets (savings, investments, or items you can convert to cash).

3. Outside funding – Draw a circle on paper labeled "Circle of Funders." In the center, list family and close friends to contact. In the next outer circle, list associates or colleagues that know you. In the outer circle list banks, lending institutions and "creative finance sources" (crowd funding, financing receivables, angel investors, community angels, etc.). Remember, you are sourced in abundance...make this an adventure and go find your funder! If you need help, contact me!

Decide to serve…not sell.

Put your clients

interests first.

Always!

~ Patricia Barnett

~*LAW NINE*~

EARN MONEY AND PROFIT
Attract the Right Customers and Serve Them Well

Patricia Barnett

In my 20 years of experience in the Direct Sales Industry I have learned that truly, the number one fear in humans is public speaking, followed closely by sales. Funny, no one wants to be a salesman/woman except salespeople themselves. The fact is that success in business requires an exchange of money for a particular product or service. The truth is you never have to sell a day in your life as long as you add value in service of others

Many times I ask business owners or people in a "sales" position, "Why would people want to work with you or buy the particular product/service from you?" The answer to this question is incredibly revealing because it becomes clear whether the person answering is "serving" or "selling." So think about that question for a moment... How would you answer it? What is it that would make your clients want to work with *you*? List your top answers.

1. _____

2. _____

3. _____

4. _____

5. _____

Not long ago, I received a call from a relatively high-end dress shop that I simply love. The gal on the other end of the phone said, "Good morning, Patricia, this is Erica from so-and-so boutique. I am calling to tell you that we have just received our newest shipment for the season. It is filled with amazing pieces that we love and that we think are the best yet. We are having an event this weekend and are inviting guests and their friends to attend so that they can see our collection. We believe it is going to be an incredible event. Also, we will have plenty of staff on hand to help you buy your wardrobe for the season from our new collection."

Please take a moment to read the above paragraph again. As you do, put yourself in my shoes as if Erica were calling you personally. What do you think and feel when you put yourself into the receiving end of this sales situation?

Here's what I was thinking...

As a customer of the boutique, my first thought was gratitude and feeling so special that the sales gal made a personal call to me. As a sales coach what I heard next was Erica's focus on herself, the store and how excited they were about their new collection. In fact, at the time of this call, I had yet to buy one new thing for the season. Even so, her invitation did not inspire, did not engage, nor did it invite a burning desire to attend the event or even buy from her. It could be that with my experience as a sales coach, I was jaded; however, what I know for sure is that had the conversation gone differently, the results would have been much different for me and, I have a feeling, for many of the others Erica called that day as well.

See it's not just experienced sales trainers who see right through "being sold"; in fact, everyone has what I call a sixth sense when *feeling sold*. There is a saying that is oh so true: "People do not care what you know (or what you have) until they know how much you care." Let me explain...

Imagine the conversation had gone more like this...

"Hello, Patricia, it's Erica from so-and-so boutique. It is a new season of fashion and I am calling to see how I can be of support to *you*. I know you are a busy professional with a high value on time and looking your best. Have you had a chance to update your closet with the styles that will take you all of the places you'll be going this season?" Had that been the question, Erica would have found out immediately that I had not realized that we were even *in* a new season.

The truth was that with my attention on my business, speaking engagements, supporting my clients along with full family and social calendar, shopping was the very last thing on my mind. I most likely would have said, "No, Erica, there have been so many wonderful things happening in my life that I haven't given it a thought." At this point, the Erica offering great *service* would say, "Patricia, we would be happy to be of support for you. We actually have just received a fantastic new shipment of amazing pieces for the new season and we would love the opportunity to work with you to create the styles that suit your needs best for all occasions coming up on your calendar. In fact, you can come in at your convenience and in a very short time our professional stylists can help you with everything you'd love to fit your needs, look your best and maximize your time getting ready each day. As a bonus, we are even hosting a fun and fabulous event. If you would like to bring a friend we'd be happy to assist you *and* your friend."

Chances are I would have welcomed a recess from my full schedule for an evening of fun and fashion, invited a few friends to attend and with the help and service of the experts, gone home with a completely new wardrobe for the season. Erica would have received commissions from my purchases *AND* my friends' purchases too.

The difference in the second example is it was all about how she could have served me best; supporting my desire for a new wardrobe with her amazing new shipment and brilliant customer service. Here's the truth: the very best sales in any industry come from the very best service.

In the scenario above, I was in need of an updated wardrobe for the season with little time to shop. In addition, I *wanted* an updated wardrobe too. If you own or work for a boutique that carries fun, fashion-forward, elegant and classic clothes with personalized attention to accommodate my schedule then you would be of great service for me because of my desire for it.

Let's take look at your current business and strategy for acquiring clients/customers. The first question in expanding your business is, "Who benefits from my product or service?" Next ask, "What are the benefits that my clients/customers will receive by means of my product and/or service?"

If you are marketing a health product that offers benefits of energy, feeling great and better sleep, then your target market could be people who have little or no energy, feel rotten and can't sleep.

If you have an income opportunity that will produce extra and/or residual income for others, then you are of great service to those who are interested in creating additional or passive income.

If you have a washing machine repair shop…you guessed it! You are in service to those who have broken washing machines.

If you have running shoes for sale then you serve runners best.

If you are a teacher you teach those who are interested in learning.

First, know how you can serve people best. Next, it is about sharing why you are the best to fill that need. First about them, second about you.

So let's ask the original question one more time. This time fill in the pain points of the clients/customers you are interested in serving.

Why would a client want to work with you?

How do your products or services benefit your clients most?

What is it that would make your clients *want* to work with *you*?

What are the top 5 answers to the questions above?

1. _____

2. _____

3. _____

4. _____

5. _____

Filling a need is being in "service." "Sales" generally happen when you are trying to get someone to "buy" something in order to benefit *you*. Think sales goals, income goals, etc. Serving is filling a need and helping someone purchase a product or service because it will be of benefit to *another*. Find out who will benefit and then serve them well. By serving well you will surpass your greatest "sales" goals. It seems so subtle at first. Yet, the difference is monumental. Whether you serve or sell - your results, income/growth, achieving goals and results will follow, not only today; for each transaction in the future.

The greatest problems and challenges I have ever had in sales personally came when selling for my gain vs. serving others for their benefit. In my early days of sales it was all about my goal, my sales and my income. I learned quickly that I was not the primary focus in order to reach my goals. By *serving* others and teaching the heart-centered leaders within our organization to do the same, it was only a very short time that I was recognized as one of the Top 20 Associate within an international company of over 200,000 sales associates and then from there entered into the prestigious Million Dollar Club.

People don't buy what they need. They buy what they *want.*

The approach above can take you anywhere you desire to go in business, in sales and in income. The challenge comes if from here you try to *serve* those in need who don't *want* your product or service.

Once you have identified the need, the next question is does this person *want* what I have. Help others discover why they would want what you know they need. Offer people solutions to their need and help them see how their life will be easier or better when they buy from you. Speak with the people who need your product and serve the ones who *want* your product and/or service.

You've heard the saying, "You can lead a horse to water, but you can't make it drink." In my business, I have seen very "thirsty horses" who are just not ready to "drink." If someone is not ready for you, bless her and then go find the ones who are. It is easy to get stuck on those who you know can benefit and who for whatever reason choose not to move forward with you. As long as you can really benefit others, know this...your future clients are EVERYWHERE. Your job is to keep moving and to attract them and them to serve them well.

Teach others on your team to do the same and then repeat this again and again and again. In addition to serving your clients well, apply the ideas in the rest of this chapter and your future will be brighter than you could have ever imagined. You will be able to write any goal you wish and then achieve and even exceed your sales goals every time.

At the end of the day, one of the simplest and most powerful questions you can ask anyone and everyone you come in contact with, in business or otherwise, is, "How can I be of service to you today?" Or stated another way, "How can I support you?" Help enough people get what they want and you will never have to worry about achieving your goals and living your dreams. Simply put, by serving others you will never have to sell a day in your life.

One word of caution: Don't confuse this type of "serving others" with charity. In serving your clients well there will be an exchange of money. Just because you are serving others does not mean there is not an exchange of money. Of course there will be an exchange of money. There is simply is no such thing as "something for nothing." The truth is there *must* be an exchange of money from your customers/clients to have the greatest benefit by means of your efforts, products and service. In the Law of Compensation it is stated your customers/clients must pay in order that they reap the greatest benefit possible.

Identify your perfect client or customer.

So, now that you know you are serving the needs of others via your product or service the next question is whom would you love as your customers and/or clients? Whether you are growing an existing business or creating a client list for the first time, it is important for you to identify who you would love to work with and the characteristics of those customers and clients. I believe that anything you are searching for already exists and is closer than you think. By focusing specifically and tuning into what you desire, you will easily find it. Once you get really clear on what you truly want, you too will see that it was there all the time.

Many times it seems like magic, as if your new customer/client appears out of the blue. It is an easy and fun process that offers great benefit for you when you engage in the activity. The power of this process does not actually come from out of the blue; it comes from *within you.*

Several years ago, there was a brand new type of car, new to the market, with a body style that had never been seen. It was about the same time that I was looking for a new car to buy. My husband had gone out of town for the weekend and while away he decided to visit a dealership to take a look at the new model. As if it were out of the blue, my husband called and said, "I think I have found the perfect car for you! It is everything you've said you wanted in a car, it's incredibly safe, spacious, tons of power, luxurious and looks really cool." He was so thrilled and told me that there was such a high demand for this new beast that none would be available for months. As luck would have it, this particular dealership had just this one left which was originally a special order. (The original buyer's wife preferred a different color, which left just this one available.)

My husband said, "If you like, I will buy it now and we can come back to pick it up this weekend." I asked my husband, "What kind of car is it?" He told me, but because it was a brand new car to the market, I had no idea of what it looked like. My husband did his best to explain. He said, "Remember last week in Hawaii, they were *everywhere!*" The more he described the car, the more frustrated I became, telling him, "No! I don't remember seeing a new style of car!" Finally, I went to our local dealer to put an end to the mystery. Upon seeing the car for the first time, I would have told you there had been *none* in my path, in Hawaii or otherwise. After a quick test drive, I knew it was the car for me. I called my husband, thrilled to say, "Yes, I would love that car!" That weekend, my husband and I drove to pick up my new ride. Within a day or two, I began to see them literally *everywhere!*

You may remember a time in your life when you experienced the same, whether it was a new car, hairstyle, product or movie star. Our brains actually help us to focus and find things, people or situations that otherwise would have been missed had we not been tuned in to that which we were in search of finding. In the Bible, it is written, "Seek and ye shall find." First, you must be clear of what you are seeking. With clear focus and attention you are sure to find it. I was clear on what I wanted in a car. Upon finding (with help from my husband) the perfect fit, it was evident that they were everywhere. The same will be true for you as you create what you want in a customer or client.

So here's the question:

What are the top 5 qualities and characteristics of the clients and customers you would love to serve? (Examples: Fun, Pays on time, Easy to work with, Teachable, Wanting results, etc.)

1. _____

2. _____

3. _____

4. _____

5. _____

Live in gratitude for your clients...past, present and future.

So now that you are clear of who you'd love to serve, here is the "miracle grow" that will expand your customer base so that it is strong and multiplies exponentially. It is only one word and is more powerful than any of us can even comprehend...it is called *GRATITUDE*. Being grateful for your business, team and clients is really one of the most important orders of business each day that you are in business.

Recently, I was visiting with dear friends and very successful business owners in Kansas City. It had been several years since I had been with them both and it was such a thrill to hear about their current business especially as they had given me the opportunity to work for them over 25 years ago. As a family business, the current owner had started the company with his father from their garage at home back in the day (over 50 years ago). Their company was built upon filling a desire for their customers while providing impeccable service. As business grew, the company grew, eventually moving to a large and efficient facility with offices, manufacturing facility and warehouse. At their new location a new proprietary product was created and business continued to increase.

As the next generation became involved in the business, expansion continued: new divisions of service, new locations, expansion of the sales team, expansion of team members and employees and increase of customers and revenue. In asking about the company today, the answer was clear. What I heard was growth, expansion and increase, as well as the recognition of far surpassing the original vision for the company in the beginning. I asked my friend, the co-founder and owner of this thriving company, "To what do you attribute your success?" The answer came to him in an instant, which he shared with me so genuinely and heartfelt, "Our customers. I am so grateful for our customers." He went on to say, "We would have never had what we had, learned what we learned, or grown to where we are today without our customers." He added, "Each day I give thanks. I am so grateful for each and every customer we've ever had, those who are with us now and for those we have yet to serve."

"Consumers, customers and clients are the lifeblood of your business. Appreciate them and your business will grow." ~ Patricia Barnett

You may have heard of something called a "Gratitude Journal." You may even have a current gratitude practice. Have you ever thought of a gratitude journal specifically for your business and/or clients? Well, here is your opportunity. Each day in giving thanks, write out your "gratitude's" for your colleagues, customers and/or clients. What I know for sure is that this one idea has the power to grow your business and transform it quickly.

Before you begin this gratitude practice, make a note of what your business looks like today. If you are really committed to growing your business, commit to writing in your gratitude journal for the next 90 days consecutively, each day giving thanks and writing your "gratitude's." As you bring your customers, clients and colleagues to mind, wish each of them well. What I know for sure is that your results will change for the better. Increased business, more customers and/or clients and increased income. We'd love to hear from you and celebrate the shifts, increases and expansion in your business and life over the next 90 days!

Email us at *results@WealthMasteryForWomen.com.*

Give! Find ways to surprise and delight your customers/clients.

It may be true that not *everyone* likes to be surprised and yet most delight in feeling valued. Now that you have a really great understanding of your consumer base, you know where they struggle or have challenges and how you can benefit them. You know the main characteristic and qualities of the base you are growing, you are grateful for them because you know that you are in business because of them. The next question is how can you add even more value to them? This is what we call "surprise and delight" because this goes above and beyond the purchase of the product or service they have paid you initially.

A surprise and delight is anything that your customers/clients do not expect in return. For sure there are things your clients expect even if it is not spelled out in your initial sales transaction. Of course your clients and customers are going to expect great customer service, because it's you who they are working with. Of course they are going to expect shipments on time and to receive products in great shape too. What they might not expect is shipping three days early or an added product sample with their order. That's what I mean by surprise and delight. Many years ago in the sales industry this was known as "underpromise and overdeliver." Surprise and delight includes underpromising, overdelivering, and yet it is so much more. It is about being thoughtful and showing your appreciation for your customers. It is about providing extra service and benefits especially when the customer/client least expects it. It is about giving!

Many times when we think of giving, we think of things as it relates to money. In workshops I will ask, "What would you love to give your clients?" Every once in a while I'll hear, "When I have clients, then I can give." Or "When I make the money, then I can think about giving." Well, here is the news. Where it is true that earning more money provides greater resources to give; money is not the only resource we have to give our customers/clients. There are endless ways to give. All you have to have is an imagination to think of ways to give.

Let's take a moment now to Mastermind some ideas for you to surprise, delight and give to your customers/clients.

For this exercise, I invite you to think of your clients for a moment. Bring a picture of them (collectively as a whole or individually) to mind. As you see the picture of them in your mind, ask the question, "What would be a great way to surprise and delight my clients?" "What can I give?" As ideas come to mind begin writing them down. As you write your ideas, more will come to you. The trick is to keep writing all of the ideas as they come. It may be tempting to say, oh, I don't like that one so I won't list it. Please list ALL of the ideas; you can edit them later.

As mentioned, your "gives" could be ideas that require money such as express delivery for product or samples of products. And yet there are so many things you can give that require very little if any money at all. You could give your clients ideas, time, additional service, referrals for their business, thoughts and prayers, discount, a card, a smile, a laugh, encouragement, email, text, special greeting or simply a smile. The list goes on and on...

What would I love to do or give that would surprise and delight my customers or clients?

_____

_____

_____

_____

_____

_____

_____

They had me at "Hello"!

One of the best surprise and delights that I have received recently was at a grocery store in the Midwest. As I walked through the door, a man greeted me with a happy and sincere "Hello, miss." There was an immediate connection with that friendly gentleman and in turn with the store itself.

Although that didn't seem like such surprise at first, as I made my way to the deli I began to see a pattern. The man behind the counter was one of the happiest deli clerks I had ever encountered. My thought, "What a happy guy!" He enthusiastically filled my order and as I left the counter, he said, "We appreciate you shopping with us. Happy to see you again soon!" My next thought was, "Wow, how nice. He was such a pleasure, I'd love to come back."

Next stop was produce. There was a woman stacking fruit who asked how my day was. I told her that each day was a gift to me and she said in return, "Ma'am, you are a gift to us. We appreciate you shopping with us!" Now I am thinking, "This entire place is filled with happy, helpful people."

As I turned the corner there was someone who greeted me to ensure that I was finding everything I needed. In asking for directions for the "gluten-free" aisle, the woman proceeded to walk with me to show me their entire "health food section" and then asked, "Is there anything else I can do to make your shopping experience even better?" I said, "No thank you, this is it for today." To which she responded, "We appreciate so much that you are here and look forward to seeing you next time." Now I am thinking, "Am I in heaven?"

This friendly service continued throughout my entire visit. From the time I walked into the store to the time I walked out, every person greeted me with appreciation and interest in having me come back. With a genuine smile on their faces and in every interaction, each *looked at me, directly in my eyes,* as if they were speaking to my heart and soul.

My experience there was a surprise because it was so different and such departure from our current culture that exists in grocery shopping, or any shopping for that matter. It was such a delight because I felt incredibly appreciated and valued as a customer. In fact, besides Disneyland, I think this might just be the "happiest place on earth." If I lived in that city, it would be my "go to" place. Not living in that city, I have shared the experience with everyone I know who lives there and I will be thrilled to visit upon returning to the Midwest. They gave me a happy and helpful place to shop. They received a happy customer who shared the experience with many others resulting in additional and continued sales. Now multiply my experience with the experience of the hundreds of customers that day (and then multiply that by 365 representing the next year) and what you will find is an absolutely thriving grocery store. And when that culture is from that store is taken nationally, the possibilities for that grocery chain is remarkable.

So let's get back to the real question at hand. What will you give? How will you surprise and delight your customers/clients? Decide now to make this a priority. Do this well and you will create a solid foundation of loyal customers/clients, expansion of business and continued growth of your consumer base for many years to come or potentially even a lifetime.

LAW NINE - ACTION STEPS

EARN MONEY AND PROFIT

Attract the Right Customers and Serve Them Well

Action Steps:

1. Decide to serve, not sell – put your clients' interests first. Always! What are the qualities and characteristics of the people you serve?
2. Live in Gratitude – create specific daily practices of gratitude for current clients and for your future clients coming to you even now. Visualize each of them and give thanks.
3. Give! – Find ways you can surprise and delight your clients, increasing the value you bring to their lives.

And of course, we have a special surprise just for you! Visit:

www.WealthMasteryforWomen.com/gift

Our actions are always perfectly aligned with our thoughts. Look deeply; you are the creator of your world.

~Marilyn Macha

~*LAW TEN*~

GROW YOUR WEALTH

Be Responsible, Reinvest, Save, and enJOY!

Marilyn Macha

Wealth is a state of being, rather than "some place to arrive." When we live a life that is truly wealthy (remember that the definition of wealth has to do with well-being and happiness), all IS well and your "being" is healthy and present. The energy of money provides a healthy exchange of value, a continuum of energy, free flowing and directed, focused. When we hoard money, fret about losing money, fear that there is not enough, those thoughts will be acted upon and will create disharmony in life.

The energy of physical vitality provides the ability to be present, to be clear in our thinking, to make good choices. Wealth is a state of being – get curious about that and ask yourself, "What's important about money?" Look at the "why" – why you even want or need money. Perhaps it is to have a nice home, nice care, be respected, take trips, buy flowers, and create beauty around you? But why?

My husband and I like to go to fine restaurants; we like to dress up, savor excellent, flavorful, nourishing foods and fine wine; it's our entertainment. We are both committed to enjoying our life together, in activities, which we both enjoy. Our commitment, though, is to our relationship and feeling nurtured in our environment, where we can converse and share ideas and dreams together. These are our evenings in fine dining. It's about nurturing our souls, our relationship and our bodies. What do you or would you love to do with your money? How do you see using your money, your resources and your physical vitality? As an exchange of value? Paying for something? And where does the idea of investing come into play?

To invest in yourself is the first vital step in growing your wealth. Part of investing in yourself is to learn, read and grow daily by looking at your thoughts; what you are thinking. Our actions, our activities are directly related to and perfectly aligned with our thoughts (always!). Get support; we're not meant to be alone. Get a mentor, a coach, someone who is trained, someone who has experience in life who will make a difference for you.

I have a friend who is about to become an "empty nester." She has been in the noble profession of being a stay-at-home mother and wife for over 20 years. With her son's moving, she openly expresses that she doesn't know what to do with or for herself. She expresses that she doesn't know what she wants to do with her life and she feels as if she's withering on the vine with nothing to live for.

This is a normal condition of thinking. But the brilliance of this awareness, this acknowledgment, is that: it is only a thought! And she is one thought away from a life that she loves living. This transition, particularly, begins with "Investing in herself"! It's as if she's on a plane having mechanical difficulties and in order to make a difference and not die, herself, she *must* put her own oxygen mask on first; she must invest in herself so that she is able to take care of others (which she has loved doing). We must teach ourselves that it's not selfish to invest in ourselves; it is vital and life enhancing, for ourselves AND for others, to invest in ourselves!

My friend's experience is an exaggerated one, perhaps, but to invest in ourselves is mandatory no matter in which stage of life we are. To seek support and coaching from one whose life we admire is a powerful asset. Her thinking, the ease and grace in which she lives life is something that we admire and desire. Invest in your health; buy organic, eat natural sugars, read books that inspire and teach, watch more shows that stimulate your thinking and invest your money. Begin wherever you are!

We all *know* to do things that improve our expression and experience of life. Why don't we do it? Why don't we do it consistently? Because our own mind will coerce to the "comfortable, easy way out" (which, over time, becomes just the opposite – illness, uncertainty, frailty, fear, worry) and without support, left to our own devices, we become seduced. This is normal for human beings. There is nothing wrong with this – AND there is a resolve for it! Get a coach who will hold you accountable and then BE accountable!

Invest time in yourself. Take classes that increase your knowledge or awareness of what you want to have in your life. Invest – not spend. Invest and Spend are defined later in this chapter.

Don't spend time doing things that take you further away from your dream, perhaps mindless video games for hours, watching shows that promote hatred, revenge, activities that take you away from believing in your desires and your ability to create. That you are still reading this book confirms that you have great desires and that you are worthy of them. Invest in you. Invest your time to your advancement. Make choices that forward you toward those desires. Before you begin to do certain activities that take time, ask yourself, "will this activity take me closer to or further away from my desired result?"

Often we will use the excuse of "I don't have the time" or "I don't have the money" about the things that would forward us in our desired results. Begin to notice when that is a habitual reaction because of the belief that "I can't really have what I want" or "I am not worthy enough, capable enough, to live that vision." With those immediate, knee jerk responses ("I don't have the time") you will begin to create the reality of not enough around you. You begin to take actions that confirm and are in alignment with and support that belief of not enough time or not enough money. Begin to notice what you tell yourself automatically. It will matter what you tell yourself.

I remember when that was an automatic response to any question asked of me to invest in myself or begin saving money or doing just about anything counter to how I was "doing" life in the moment. It takes something to change a thought pattern, and investing...in yourself, in your company (or your relationship *with* a company as an employee) or into an investment account itself. This is the first stage of Growing Your Wealth. Growing by Investing.

What does it mean to INVEST: to put money to use in something offering potential returns (interest, income, appreciation in value), rather than SPEND: to pay out, expose of. When you invest in yourself you can see in your mind the future value of what the purchase enhances, or the way of being, or the expanding thought process. And when you're quiet, pensive about the action step, the activity, the decision, you *know*.

Early on in my independence, being on my own for the first time after my divorce, I bought a small patio home for my son and me (great investment, well priced, good terms, payments in alignment with my earnings at the time, trained me in "committed to my well-being") and then I bought a solar panel for the house (convinced by the sales team that it would enhance the value of my home; I didn't have the money, borrowed it from my mother, and knew, even then, in my heart, that I was buying it "because it was a good deal; they discounted it for "me'" (I felt special) and it meant to me that I was showing the world that "I was more than what I had." That is NOT investing; that was spending! When you get quiet, you will know; I didn't know at the time how important it was to listen to my inner knowing rather than spend money on something that would make me look better than I felt about me.

You already do have a pattern of spending. What are you putting your attention on? Look at your checkbook, bank statements and your credit card invoices. The first step in this stage of the *12 Laws* is to look and *see* what you are spending money on; is it really where you want to put your money? Or is it just an old habit; a default pattern? We can only up-level, improve, transform that which we are willing to look at, observe, and really see what's so.

Investing is a different mind-set. We use this term, intuitively, when we refer to time and/or money. Am I spending time, am I spending money...or am I investing that same amount of time or money? "I spent so much time on that project" (indicates that "I" wasn't' invested IN the project...it was just something to get completed. Doesn't it even feel different to say "investing money" or "spending money"? Try it on...say it out loud...

There are tools and structures to apply when we begin to understand how our thoughts will create our results. Our thoughts and our beliefs about ourselves, how the world works, how people *are*, and those thoughts will dictate our actions. That action dictates another's actions and the world keeps showing up the same way over and over. In order to change our outcome we must begin with a new thought. It was Einstein who said, "We cannot solve our problems with the same thinking we used when we created them." It is mandatory, therefore, in preparing ourselves for an adventure of a new life, for us to pause, reread the first nine Laws and realize that those nine Laws have paved the way for a new way of life.

This Law is where "the rubber meets the road"; where I come face to face with myself and ask: "Am I willing to take the actions necessary to implement what I am learning? And if so, am I willing to do it daily, consistently, repeatedly?"

Being willing doesn't guarantee that you won't take an action step that will not support your growth in being wealthy, but it does mean that you will catch it and make the appropriate alterations. A continuous question to ask is, "Will this action regarding money move me toward my desire to be wealthy or move me further away?"

I was at a garden center recently and found an orchid plant on sale (a very good price for the orchid). Oh, I wanted to buy it; after all, it was *only* $10! I put it in my basket. I paused and, having learned to pay attention to what I'm thinking (which is reflected in how my body is feeling), I noticed that I wasn't calm or peaceful or joyous about the lovely orchid. I was going out of town for a week the following week and afterward I would be away from the house for an entire month. I tried to justify the purchase because it was "only ten dollars." I put the orchid back on the shelf. That $10 was to be invested in a better investment.

If you remember anything about this section, this Law of Growing Your Wealth, remember this: How you treat $10 (or a dime) is how you will treat $1,000. We cannot be one way with a small amount of money and different with a large amount of money. In the realm of energy (and money is an energy form; everything is energy) there is no big or small; it's simply energy. Treat your money with respect. It takes care of you; it is there for you. It does not make you a better person. You are not a great person (or a bad one) because you have money (or don't have money). The only way money is a reflection of you is that you get to see, in physical reality, what you think about money in relation to yourself. What I mean by that is that if you're making money to give you importance, you will struggle, because the amount of money you have will wax and wane; it is impermanent. Who YOU are is magnificent; no amount of money will make you bigger or lesser.

If you think that you have to have money to be important then your importance will be measured by how much money you have. It's backwards: you will have as much money as you think that you are worthy of. If you think that your worth is based on what you have, you will continue to struggle with keeping it, fear losing it and it will run you. Money is there FOR your care; it does not give you meaning!

This type of thinking creates binges, just like a drunk – when we don't feel good about ourselves, we either spend more than we have (credit card debt, etc.) or hang onto it so tightly that we fear having life itself without money.

Take a deep breath. Tying these last two paragraphs together I ask the question: What does this idea have to do with the Growth of Wealth? We must begin to build new practices – and that's where investing, rather than spending (or hoarding, at the opposite end of the same spectrum) comes in. Investing is a practice to do for yourself because you respect and honor yourself; that you are more interested in what you imagine, what you love, what you desire (a "Burning Desire" as Napoleon Hill called it) than you are in your old patterned way of thinking and "doing" life. So often, it takes being fed up with the way "it is."

Investing is different from saving. Investing is a natural action step from within. Saving is typically earmarked for a particular want or event (a Christmas savings account). Saving for retirement is not as empowering as investing in a life "I" would love living for the rest of my life. I don't know about you, but I don't ever see me "retiring" – retiring from life? Retiring from my job, my business, my work in the world? Perhaps "leave" a job because it's not what I love or am now "complete" with that phase of my life...but retire from something that I love? I think not...

Let me bring that back now to investing in your business – whether or not *you* own the business. If you're putting your energy into a company, it's yours. Treat it with respect (or go somewhere else). That is the beginning of investing in your business. Invest your time, your thoughts, your contribution with reverence. Be deliberate in *how* you think about what you are doing professionally. If you're there just to bring home a paycheck, your paycheck will reflect that. If you're a contribution to others at the business, to the clients or customers, your own "wealth" will appreciate. Investing provides appreciation – literally and figuratively.

If you own your own business, invest in its growth, just like your personal growth. Up-level technology, reward with bonuses, be compassionate and generous with your employees, vendors, even the mail carrier. Your results are a direct reflection of your attitude, your generosity, your passion for the business you're in.

In 1995 I incorporated my then investment advisory "practice." It occurred to me that I wanted "to be a part of something bigger than me." It became a relationship for/to which I could develop, love, nurture to empower those with whom I served in my field. I began investing IN the business. I "took home" less than before, for a while. AND that investment paid off. I continue to receive income from the business, having sold it to a qualified, dedicated buyer. It continues to reward me.

Know that there is enough – there is always "enough." Look for its evidence; you will find it. If you look from fear, you will find "enough of not enough." It is ALL there, always: enough and not enough. How will you interpret and interact with "enough"? We find and take action steps and experience from the evidence of what we look for. This is neurological, it is scientific; we get what we focus on. We GET what we FOCUS on! This is the good news. When you can see upon what your focus is gazed, YOU have the ability to shift your focus.

When you focus on the "enoughness," you will naturally know and take action toward investing consistently and systematically into your own investment account. Even if it's $25 a week, or $25 a month, begin it!

As W. H. Murray wrote: "Whatever you can do, or dream you can, begin it. Boldness has genius, power, and magic in it."

And Nike: Just DO IT!

The ease will come as you develop your belief in knowing that all is well. As you notice your thoughts, you now have choice. When you are aware of your choice of thoughts, the direction you are allowing your thoughts to go, you begin to have the potential of making a new choice. The human brain is the only brain that can make choices and shift the focus of their thoughts. As you awaken to the life you love, you begin to make different choices and out of every new choice is a new action. And every action begins to produce a different result, a new life.

This is where most people stop; but not you. That you had the desire to pick up this book and read it, the next step is to apply what you are learning, to your own life. Find a mentor who has experienced what you desire and ask them for support. Be courageous and willing to think newly (if you want new results, invest in you, in your business...which IS you, anyway) and take the action step of "putting your money where your mouth is" (not sure I even know what that means, except to say, DO what you said that you'd do!! It is to Grow Your Wealth!!)

Then take Investment steps in alignment with that belief. It's lucrative, it's empowering, and it's a whole lot of fun!!!

LAW TEN - ACTION STEPS

GROW YOUR WEALTH

Be Responsible, Reinvest, Save, and enJOY!

Action Steps:

1. Invest in yourself – Actively participate in self-development and coaching regularly. Nurture yourself with what you love: bike rides, walks, massages, at least four times a month.

2. Invest in your business – Put money toward updating your systems and equipment, and exceed expectations by rewarding your staff and clients with bonuses, surprises and acknowledgment. Believe in what you provide (if you don't, don't do it!), be grateful for all that you have and are providing and give generously in thought, word and deed.

3. Invest in your future – Put monthly amounts in an investment account. The percentage does not matter as much as simply beginning the process and watching $50 a month grow to $100 a month and on and on. Have a "numbers goal" in mind for the year's contribution, a five-year cumulative amount, etc. Make it a fun game and trust that your commitment to yourself and "what the money provides" grows. Typically, if your "investment account" is just

beginning, a bank savings account will work. Once you pass $15,000 talk to a financial planner at the bank and look at conservative mutual funds. Six figures and above, begin asking friends and relatives, co-workers, for the name of a trusted financial advisor. Interview several...and trust your intuitive barometer telling you with whom to invest. Have FUN knowing that you are taking care of you, your business and your family. The energy of money supports life. Grow with it!

Go into the world and learn about your sisters and brothers. Walk down their streets, sit in their homes, eat their food, laugh and cry with them.

This leads to understanding. Understanding leads to love. And love leads to peace on earth

~ Paula Fellingham

~*LAW ELEVEN*~

EXPAND AND GO GLOBAL
Collaborate and Share Your Message Worldwide

Paula Fellingham

I will begin Law Eleven with a piece I wrote recently that describes what I believe is the GREATEST STRATEGY and KEY to expanding and "going global." This strategy, and key to success, is collaboration.

Collaboration: The Model That Works in the 21st Century

To best address our growing social, political and economic problems, I believe humanity needs to incorporate the Collaboration Model in the 21st century, rather than continue with the age-old Dominance Model, if we are to move away from poverty and war and toward prosperity and peace.

The Collaboration Model has as its highest priority the caring for people. Its focus is the creation of mutually beneficial relationships.

Simply stated, the Dominance Model is about top-down control and the Collaboration Model is about creating healthy, sustainable relationships. The first is based on the need to dominate and control; the second is based on the ability to trust and collaborate.

Historically, humanity has been subjected most often to the Dominance Model. Why? Because power and riches usually go to those who dominate, whereas trusting collaborators are generally open, vulnerable and at risk of being dominated by their partners.

Since the Dominance Model is top-down, like nation over nation, religion over religion, man over woman, examples include any relationship or system where domination occurs. Since domination has been a consistent theme throughout history, those of us living in the 21st century can easily look back and agree that this model is not conducive to peace. On the contrary, the Dominance Model causes, rather than discourages, conflict and war.

I believe at this critical time in history the world needs more people who are willing to create collaborative relationships based on mutual respect and mutual benefit. Additionally, more equalitarian relationships (relationships based on equal rights) are needed today in our families, in our businesses and in our governments. Those who understand and practice these models will surge forward successfully, and those who do not, will not.

As with most things that are beautifully simple, collaboration begins with our thoughts, our attitudes and the questions we ask ourselves.

Those who think abundantly ask, "How can I help you?" and/or "How can we help each other?" before asking, "What's in it for me?" They who ask such questions have the best chance of succeeding with the Collaboration Model in their personal relationships and in their businesses.

People who genuinely desire to create mutually beneficial relationships authentically seek to create win-wins. The good news is that those who aren't naturally inclined to think abundantly can easily be taught to do so. It's a matter of wanting to learn a more effective way of being, then acquiring the tools and practicing until old "dominance" thoughts, habits and patterns are changed.

Succeeding with the superior Collaboration Model is about being "others-centered" rather than "self-centered." Others-centered leaders work to find ways to make life better for those in their circles of influence. Self-centered leaders work to find ways to make their own lives easier and better. Their genuine concern for the welfare of others is low or non-existent. Through the ages, benevolent leaders have been revered and dominant leaders have been feared.

One of the things I learned from my friend Riane Eisler *(Roadmap to a New Economics)* is that if we are to create new, more sustainable and equitable relationships and systems that have the power to dissolve anger, discontent, and inequality worldwide, we must discuss the roots of the problems. We must go deep into matters that statisticians, theorists and conventional economic analyses often ignore. We must discuss basic values and human needs that are often minimized or ignored in the Domination Model that prevails, in varying degrees worldwide, across all "isms" of government (capitalism, socialism, communism) and across all types of relationships and businesses.

A healthy, open discussion about values and human needs is prerequisite to moving the world from the prevailing Dominance Model to the superior, and much needed, Collaboration Model. Since we are co-creators of our problems (as co-inhabitants on this planet) it behooves us to discuss solutions together.

The first step to creating Global Collaboration might be cross-country discussions about how individuals and nations can collaborate for mutual benefit. We're talking about developing partnerships on a massive scale. Can this be done? Absolutely! Why will it work? Because at the end of the day the Human Family does care about the same things: prosperity and peace.

So to all who believe that creating mutually beneficial relationships are superior to top-down control... to those who believe that caring for people should be a high priority for lawmakers, let's dialogue.

Let's begin by talking about which basic values and human needs should be part of a society based on the Collaboration Model.

Caring (by definition) suggests we consider all life as valuable. It follows, then, that the life of a child is far more valuable than stocks or bonds. And if we believe that our children and families are more valuable than financial instruments, our economic policies and practices should reflect that. Societies should insist on practices that encourage health and good education for all. Policies created should encourage such things as individual and national productivity; financial and economic sustainability.

Are not our values skewed when massive money is spent on warfare and rockets while masses of people suffer because their basic needs are not met?

If we believe that the real wealth of the world lies in the contributions of humanity, then caring for people should be our highest priority. And Laws that promote human development should be created at all levels of all governments as natural outgrowths of those beliefs.

If you believe in these principles then an appropriate question is, "What's next?" And a congruent action step is to gather with those who care deeply about the future and are willing to:

1. Create in-country roundtable discussions where participants of varying social and economic status meet and discuss solutions within the context of the Collaboration Model.

2. Dialogue among nations at semi-annual conferences where every country is represented.

3. Create grassroots and government support for the Collaboration Model.

The obvious challenge with discussions that involve participants from different backgrounds and cultures is the problem of differing perspectives. Indeed, the gap between the haves and have-nots, cultural differences, religious differences, etc., pose a threat to the success of the proposed roundtable discussions and international dialogues. However, if participants can agree on long-term goals such as prosperity and peace, healthy discussions about how to accomplish those goals can include the elements of collaboration.

Old thinking assumes that top-down control will inevitably continue, but history proves that model is broken. New thinking leads to partnerships and to policies that value people and their needs. And that model works. It's time for new thinking.

I believe that the individuals, families, businesses, and nations that adopt and adhere to the Collaboration Model will not only enjoy increased prosperity, they will help lift the level of love and peace on earth in powerful ways, never before witnessed in the history of the world.

I will now share the methods I used to expand one of my companies into many nations, very quickly, using collaboration. I know, firsthand, that these methods work. When you follow these strategies you can enjoy great success "going global."

C   Choose your WIN-WIN worldwide. Begin with the end in mind and know how you can help your potential partner/collaborator and know exactly what you need from the partnership.

     Ask yourself, "How can what I have help this person or their organization?" And ask, "Exactly what do I want out of this partnership?"

O   Only choose partners who align with your heart and mission. (State mission; discuss the "e's" – education, enlightenment, entrepreneurship – and the purposes....)

L   Look to create a relationship with your partners. This means connecting heart-to-heart with them. Become friends with them. Know them. When you're communicating with them, make it real; be authentic.

I   believe that the most important part of creating a relationship is to have a servant's heart; to TRULY care about them and their success, and to proactively look for ways to help them succeed.

L   Listen carefully.

What do your partners really want and need?
Don't make assumptions. Listen with your whole heart, with a pure intent to really understand.

A   Always and sincerely look for ways to help them reach their goals.

It has been my experience that rising tides really DO float all boats; that as you help them you cannot help being blessed yourself.

B   Be crystal clear on your mutual objectives.

Define your objectives – for ALL partners and collaborators – with your Executive Team. Have these objectives written out, with a timeline for achievement.

O   Originate, or orchestrate a mutually beneficial written Agreement. Insist on mutual accountability with a clear understanding of progress timelines.

R   Record your progress and communicate frequently; bi-monthly via email and monthly via Skype or phone.

A   Appoint someone to follow up with each partner; it doesn't need to be you – but healthy, frequent, open, honest communication is critically important in ALL relationships – with your family members AND your business partners.

T   Try to give more than expected.

This is another principle that's important on many levels. Giving more than expected in ALL relationships is a key to success.

I   Ignore distractions.

This is one of the biggest challenges for successful entrepreneurs. We have SO many ideas – so many ways we can apply our skills – SO many potential partners and collaborators. Like me, is ignoring distractions a challenge for you?

Most of us sometimes hear little voices in our heads whispering things like, "Oh, THAT'S a good idea! I'll sell my products like that!" Or, "Oh, look how he's marketing that – I should do it THAT way!" And we sometimes get distracted from the goals and timelines we and our Teams set. Those who move forward toward their goals with laser focus are more likely to reach them. (Allowing, of course, for creative improvements, as necessary, along the way.)

O   Open your heart to the possibility of creating more and greater collaborations and partnerships.

N   (Winston Churchill's quote) "Never, never, never give up." Never stop doing good. Never stop giving your very best efforts to fulfilling your mission and life's purpose.

LAW ELEVEN - ACTION STEPS

EXPAND AND GO GLOBAL

Collaborate and Share Your Message Worldwide

Action Steps

1. Truly understand what it means to "Go Global" by researching potential collaborators worldwide and then discuss going global with people who have taken their businesses into numerous countries.

2. With your team, create a Global Growth Plan. Begin by listing individuals and companies with whom you want to do business worldwide. Then, create a timeline for contacting them/doing business with them. Work on systematic expansion and discuss the effectiveness of your Global Growth Plan quarterly.

3. Find international contacts in a variety of ways such as attending global conferences/industry conferences, searching for (and contacting) similar businesses and like-minded individuals. Constantly research, then reach out and connect with individuals with whom you can collaborate. Always look for ways to create WIN-WINS and use strategies that truly benefit your collaborators, grow your relationships, and expand your business. Additionally, you should constantly network and ask friends and acquaintances for international contacts in your industry, while generously sharing your contacts with others.

Discover your strength, gifts and talents, they are right where you are. It is then you will discover you have even more than you realize.

~ Julie Jones Hamilton

~LAW TWELVE~

PRACTICE THE LAW OF COMPENSATION

Discover the Gifts of Giving and Receiving

Julie Jones Hamilton

"One of the most positive transitions you can make is from viewing your work as a job to viewing it as a calling."

~Marianne Williamson

No matter what is happening in your lives, you are the one who chooses how you wish to think about it. You have one hundred percent dominion over the thoughts you choose to think. The greatest gift you give yourselves is to be willing to change your mind. No matter what the conditions may appear to be, you have the power to believe that anything is possible and that your situations could change.

Anyone can use the Law of Compensation to lift yourself out of the place you are in and into the place where you rightfully belong, the place of success and prosperity.

However, this requires you to change, and when you do your affairs will change too. You may have heard the quote by

Mahatma Gandhi, "Be the change you wish to see in the world." If it is your desire to create success in your life and in your business, you must first align yourself with the Law of Compensation.

What is the Law of Compensation? It is a Law much like the Law of Nature, Law of Reap and Sow or the Law of Cause and Effect, which cannot be changed; it must be obeyed. It is the principle in which "what we give we will receive" or "like water, we find our true level." Our thoughts and actions, guided by our desires and our will, manifest as a cause and effect, action and reaction, positive and negative. Every act has a consequence and there must be perfect balance between the two.

This Law keeps up the balance and establishes equilibrium, harmony and peace. You will notice that the Law of Compensation is operating beautifully everywhere in the phenomena of Nature. We see it in the change of seasons. No one can defy this immutable and irresistible Law. So, if you do a good act you will reap good benefits; if you do an unjust act you will sooner or later experience the consequence.

This Law is beautifully illustrated in my client experience. Michelle owned a very well-known thriving catering business for twenty-eight years and decided to sell it to create a holistic retreat center on a family farm covered in a forest of foliage, a perfect piece of land. Her father already began to build a beautiful building perfect for the center, but he was aging and unable to complete it. With her impeccable taste and style, and with the sale of her catering business Michelle knew exactly what was needed. Her desire was to invest her time and resources from the sale of her catering company into the retreat.

Her key employee considered buying her business and spent several years looking over the possibility, which looked promising. As Michelle expected to hear his final offer, he changed his mind. Declining her offer he opened his own competing catering business, even obtained her head chef, some of her customers and contracts.

It was then Michelle transformed what could have been bitterness and resentment into support and serving the higher good. Wishing her employee well, even referring business to him, she shifted her focus and made welcome new buyers. Michelle focused on the creation of her holistic center and giving the very best service in her catering business.

Eighteen months later a new buyer offered her the full asking price, bought her business and paid her extra for her work during the transition, which happened to be the exact amount needed to finish the holistic center! Michelle is convinced that by blessing her employer and blessing the potential buyer of her company, the Law of Compensation was revealed with new owners and the resources to realize her dream.

Michelle is now the proud owner of a magical holistic retreat center she is currently, delightfully renovating. She made a choice to align with the Law of Compensation, which works perfectly and continuously every time.

It is known that in the seventeenth century the scientist Sir Isaac Newton discovered a universal law, which states that for every action there is an equal and opposite reaction. This is the Law of Compensation. It not only applies to physical science but to our everyday lives in many ways. In our vital life force every thought and action has an equal and opposite reaction, even though there may be a time separation between the two.

This is of major importance when it comes to the thoughts we think and the actions we take.

Here are some questions to ask yourself: "Am I satisfied with the thoughts I think? Am I receiving the rewards of my efforts? Are my actions in alignment with what I would love to see in my life? Would I be willing to change my thoughts and behavior? Do I feel my own good is coming to me?"

Your answers will measure where you are now and where you would like to be.

When we perform our work to the very best of our ability, and we do it well, it brings out the best in us and we grow more confident, capable and efficient. Our sense of accomplishment expands.

However, when we compare our work or have negative thoughts towards our selves or others, it brings up fear, scarcity and a sense of, "I'm not good enough." Doubt and fear live in judgment, attachment and resistance to what is. Practice being non-judgmental, non-attached and non-resistant to what is unfolding before you. Know that we live in a perfect orderly universe and build your muscles in trusting this truth and the still small Voice within. Place your focus upon the present moment and upon the next right thought and action. This will allow you to feel better about yourself and become more successful.

The key to Wealth Mastery is in filling your mental attitude with the feelings of success, gratitude and happiness in the knowing that all is well and evolving in perfect order. Naturally, if you entertain thoughts of fear, lack, shame and doubt you will attract more of the same. So pay attention to what you are paying attention to. Fill your mind with thoughts, visions and ideas of success, abundance, happiness and optimism and you will be compensated with positive experiences in your daily activities.

BE A WOMAN OF INCREASE

Acknowledging the good that you already have in your life is the foundation for all abundance.
~Eckhart Tolle

You cannot stop your good from coming to you if you bless the good you already have and you give freely. Great success comes to those who always make it a habit to put more into life than they take out. They do more than they are paid to do and they are always looking for opportunities to exceed expectations. They often give more of themselves and of their resources. Notice how they are in turn rewarded with the esteem of their clients, customers and financial flow. They are in alignment with their own personal success. Your rewards will always be in direct proportion to your core values and in your service to others.

So how could you increase the value of your services to your customers, employees and family? By increasing the value of your contribution with your words, thoughts and deeds!

Increase is what everyone seeks in life. Being a woman of increase is sharing from your heart and putting your whole mind into present action, giving of yourself in gratitude and appreciation to your life and business. This may be done in an instant with a smile, a compliment or a lending hand. When you give more of yourself in value, without expecting anything in return, with everyone you deal with you become a woman of increase. You can convey this impression by holding the image of being a woman of increase and believing in yourself as you evolve in your business and in your personal affairs. This allows your belief to permeate your every action.

In order to receive your good in your business, as Wallace Wattles says in his book, *The Science of Getting Rich*, "One must pass from the competitive mind to the creative mind." As you begin the practice of gratitude and giving, you begin to activate your creativity, which then activates a stream of abundance, ideas and prosperity. Start by arranging your affairs so that you may receive your good when it comes to you. Be prepared by having your business and house in order. Suit up and show up by being the very best you can be. Your thoughts of being a woman of increase will bring to you the ideas and the business that you want and by your actions you will receive them.

Another powerful way of activating the Law of Compensation and becoming a woman of increase is to recognize and bless all that you have with a grateful heart. Bless everything in your awareness right here and now. Bless the thoughts of the success and the vision of the life you hold in your mind. Bless the desires that flow from your heart. Bless your clients and business associates. Bless your life, your gifts and talents. Bless and be grateful for your family, friends and community. Blessings activate the Law of Compensation and your good will find its way to you.

Create a *Blessing Inventory*. List and as many blessings as you can see in your life now. When you act in a grateful and expectant way for all of your good, in all of your endeavors, you will open the flow of a greater receiving.

However, you must act NOW. There is only the NOW. You cannot act in the past, nor can you act in the future. Being fully present in this moment is ALL we have.

Begin to create the reception of what you desire. Hold, with faith and purpose, the vision of yourself in your successful business and successful life. Act within your present environment with all your heart and the faith that you are creating the business success you desire now. This isn't wishful thinking. This is conscious focus. It is a disciplined daily practice that radiates a higher vibration, a higher energy frequency, which will attract to you people, situations and things out of the blue to guide and support you.

We live in a unified field of energy. The earth is surrounded by this magnetic field. *Everything* in and on this planet vibrates at an energetic rate: the animal kingdom, the plant kingdom and all of humanity. You have the capacity to raise your vibrational frequency by your focus. So focus on what gives you life and the thoughts that allow you to feel good.

When you focus on what you would love to be, do, have and give in your business and in your life, you will then see whatever you are focusing on begins to show up, sometimes in unexpected ways. They must, it's the Law. However, a word of caution: this works the same with unwanted things and negative thoughts as well. It is of the utmost importance to notice what you're noticing and where you are placing your attention.

Thoughts are energy. Each thought you hold attracts another corresponding thought, be it positive or negative, which creates a vibration. When you notice what you are noticing you can then choose which thoughts allow you to feel good, which will then raise your vibration. Everything, which is like your vibrational thought energy or frequency, will be attracted to you. This is how the Law works. It's a science called quantum physics.

You have the power to be the generator of your vibrational frequency by the thoughts you choose to think. You can generate success, wealth and abundance in a life and business you love by noticing what you are noticing and purposely choose thoughts, which give you life and allow you to feel good. This could make all the difference in your business and in your life. We invite you to be vigilant in this process. You deserve the desires in your heart; they were put there in your heart for you to experience. Become a woman of increase by being conscious of where you place your attention and radiate a higher frequency by monitoring your thought to those of success, wealth and abundance. You are meant to be wealthy and share your good with the world!

Here are 5 examples of being a woman of increase.

1. **Give the resources you can spare** to someone who needs them and then pretend you never had them.

2. **Forgive someone who wronged you** because you have compassion for them, not because they owe you.

3. **Tell someone you believe in their potential**, even if you don't receive the same support.

4. **Tell someone how you feel about them**; be vulnerable to let them know they are loved and not alone.

5. **Give your full attention to the person in front of you** even when tempted to let your thoughts wander; show them their words are valuable.

Discover the Law of Compensation by Giving and Receiving

"I have found that among its other benefits, giving liberates the soul of the giver." ~Maya Angelou

Let's talk about the most obvious forms of giving... tithing.
Tithing is a system that activates the Law of Compensation when applied deliberately. Many people tithe by emotion; however, when a system of 10% is earmarked in your income, or in your business, and delivered to a cause that is in alignment with your core values, this eliminates emotional responses.

A practice in offering a tithe is to do so to something which you believe will allow more freedom in the world or a cause that is near and dear to your heart or business.

Many people offer tithes out of guilt, pressure, and emotions to everything and everyone who asks, which may be often. When tithing is done in a deliberate manner it then becomes a regular way of consciously doing business.

Now, occasional gifting to an organization or agency when asked, especially when your personal or business mission is in alignment with the "*ask,*" may be an exception.

Check your motives when tithing. Sometimes we give because we see others doing so and we would like to feel included; this could be an emotional give. Question the reason why you are tithing. Remember, we are creating a practice of disciplined, authentic understanding for success in our business and life.

Applying the principle of tithing to your overall business strategy will ensure a continual stream of abundant energy flow.

There are three ways to tithe: Time, Talent and Treasure

- **Time.** The tithing of time is voluntarily being in service to others or an organization. It's showing up being a woman of increase. Everyone could use a helping hand and there are opportunities in every community.

Search your local area, businesses and community to share your gifts and talents. Become willing to participate and enjoy in the experience of gifting and sharing your time in this manner. You may be surprised at the hidden benefits you end up receiving when you give the commodity of your time.

List 5 ways you could give of your TIME:

1. _____

2. _____

3. _____

4. _____

5. _____

Talent. Everyone has endeavors they love to do. We are all born with a unique set of gifts and talents. What are yours? Take the time to explore what it is you feel you are good at doing. If you lean into the feeling of the things you love to do, things that give you life, therein lies the clues to your gifts and talents.

You may have a skill that may be needed right next door with a family member or at a local place of worship. There may be a talent you could perform that could make someone's life easier. When we are aware of the possibilities we have to offer and we share this with others, the Universe opens up the avenues for us to express and experience our good.

Be aware of the opportunities by being awake to sharing the best of yourself with others. It is an awareness that not only brings about more happiness and business opportunities but also allows our abundance to expand.

List 5 ways you could give of your TALENTS:

1. _____

2. _____

3. _____

4. _____

5. _____

Treasures. We all could tithe 10% of that of which we own. If you look at finances as a current of flowing energy coming in and going out, we then see how this energy is always in circulation. Much like the bloodstream in our body is ever circulating so is the circulation of the energy of money. If tithing 10% means you will have no food on the table or not enough to pay the rent, then adjust the percentage of your tithe to 5%. The idea here is to stay in the practice of tithing with whatever percentage you decide and to then grow into the 10% model.

In the acknowledgment of abundance and in the initiation of tithing you are making a commitment to the circulation of the greater good in your life and the lives of others. The unlimited Universal Energy is the supply of the abundance in this world and rewards the continual flow of circulation. There is a never-ending flow of good waiting for you to enjoy. As a rule of thumb, when giving back to the Universe a 10% tithe of what you are given, you will then be the steward of 90%, which belongs to you.

You may then decide to divide the 90%, which belongs to you. If so, it would look like this: 10% for your investments, 10% for your savings and 10% for taxes, which leaves the remaining finances to be used for your expenses.

This becomes the formula and business strategy of tithing. Treasures could be measured by money or anything of value to you when you consider tithing. Look around you. You may have something of value you are no longer utilizing. This may be considered treasures to others who are in need.

List 5 ways you could give of your TREASURES:

1. _____

2. _____

3. _____

4. _____

5. _____

We are all here to grow, give and celebrate a wealthy, vibrant and abundant life. It starts with making a decision to be the best version of YOU that you can be in any given moment. Trust, that as you give, you too shall receive.

Success and wealth is an everyday, in the moment, living reality. Each day we have the chance to make every choice an opportunity for success. We become the choices we make. Each choice defines us and creates the pathways of our life. We are always one choice away from a new beginning and experience. Choose to give your very best in all that you do and watch as providence shows up to support you.

LAW TWELVE - ACTION STEPS

PRACTICE THE LAW OF COMPENSATION

Discover the Gifts of Giving and Receiving

Action Steps

1. Be the change you want to see.

   By embodying successful thoughts and action you attract success, by embodying loving thoughts and action you attract more love, and by embodying giving thoughts and action you attract abundance. Become the image first in thought and mind, then in action and what you seek will be attracted to you. Hold the vision of your desires. Act as if it's already yours. If you want more peace become more forgiving. If you want more tolerance, become more understanding. It is up to you to be the very best version of yourself you can be.

2. Take action.

   All actions begin with you. It is your birthright to be wealthy, happy and successful. Nothing hinders you except your thoughts and nothing limits you except your fears.

The only things that control you are your beliefs. So, believe in yourself, in your intuition and this abundant Universe.

Take the time to be calm, reflective and meditative. Listen to the still small voice of your higher insight. Begin now to trust in your dreams and your desires. They belong to you; there is a reason they are in your heart. When you trust them, and trust in the process, you grow muscles in faith; faith being the ingredients of gratitude. With a grateful heart your good will come to you.

Bless and be grateful for all that you have. Give freely of yourself and your gifts and talents. Shine your inner light of love to all those far and near. And by all means, create a daily gratitude list and continue to be grateful daily.

3. Practice being a woman of increase.

What could you do to enhance every engagement? Give more of value in every transaction from saying "Hello" or giving someone a smile, offering more value with each transaction. Allow others to feel your sincere desire to increase the good on this planet by being your true lovely, genuine and authentic self. Do this for no other reason than to expand the kindness in your heart and you will then become a woman of increase with poise and calm confidence. In being *all you can be* in every moment you change your life, change your business and change the world.

Make welcome your good, your business, and your loving relationships by taking one action step, one baby step, each day in the direction of your dream! You are born with everything inside of you to create true wealth, and by applying the 12 Absolute Laws to Create Wealth; you will unlock the door to what is already yours and you can begin right now, *starting today!*

In Conclusion

"The biggest adventure you can take is to live the life of your dreams."

Oprah Winfrey

We invite you to embody *Wealth Mastery* and join us in living your absolute best life by deciding to be wealthy. Create a vision of a business and life you love living and allow your "WHY" to become your guide and your passion.

Identify your *wealth within* and gather your team or your "Favorite 5" to surround and support you. Then create a firm business plan with funding, financing and systems in place to attract to you the business, clients and customers you desire.

When your clients arrive, serve them well with profound gratitude for your business and life as you grow your wealth by developing a wealthy mindset while collaborating with others.

Learn to stretch and expand by investing in yourself, your business and your dream. Think BIG. GO global! The world needs you and what you have to offer!

Intentionally become a woman of increase by thinking higher thoughts, which will raise your energetic frequency and attracted to you people and things, which will bless and prosper you. Prepare the reception to receive your greater good by the actions outlined in this book.

This is your life. This is your time. Wealth Mastery is calling you.

Feel our arms wrapped around you, giving you hugs and supporting you along the way. As women, we are all here in this moment, now, to honor and serve one another. Together, we increase the level of peace, prosperity and love throughout the entire world. It begins with a decision, *starting today*!

Gifts and Resources

We celebrate you for taking the steps toward creating real wealth in your life. It is our pleasure to present you with this complimentary *Wealth Mastery Gift for Women* – 12 Audio Series of additional ideas, insights and tips to further support you to create wealth *starting today!*

Wealth Mastery Gift for Women–12 Part Audio Series

Visit www.WealthMasteryforWomen.com/gift

Extra Bonus!

Each of us has a personal gift especially for you!

~Paula Fellingham~

Free Video Presentation and eBook
Total Life Excellence
www.PaulaFellingham.com and click on "Free Gift."

~Patricia Barnett~

Free Audio
The Vital 7 - Essential Elements to Create a Vision that Works for YOU!
www.PatriciaBarnett.com/TheVital7

~Julie Jones Hamilton~

Free SUCCESS Toolkit
Discover Your Hidden Treasures
www.JulieJonesHamilton.com/your-free-gift/

~Lynn Kitchen~

Free Multi-Media eBook
From Dream to Table - Your Five Course Dream Experience
www.LaunchMoxie.com/lynn-kitchen-cafe-of-dreams/

~Marilyn Macha~

Free Book
Real Wealth Revealed - Awake: The Secret Logic of Becoming Rich.
www.MarilynMacha.com/WealthMasteryBonus

To view the entire *Wealth Mastery for Women* library, programs, workshops and resources available for your continued growth and success visit us at:

www.WealthMasteryforWomen.com

We value your thoughts and ideas of how we can be of even greater service to you. Please feel free to email us at:
results@WealthMasteryforWomen.com

Paula Noble Fellingham

Recipient, Doctorate of Education in Human Relations.

Internationally-acclaimed speaker and the author of six books, including the well-known Believe It! Become It! How to Hurdle Barriers and Excel Like Never Before.

Recipient of the prestigious "Points of Light Award" given by President George W. Bush. Recipient of the "President's Volunteer Service Award" given by President Barack Obama.

Honored as Washington State Young Mother of the Year and State Woman of the Year.

Currently, Dr. Paula Fellingham is the Founder and CEO of the Women's Information Network (WIN) an online educational and social network for women and a global community of women in many countries. See www.WomensInformationNetwork.com.

WIN hosted the largest gathering of women in the history of the world for International Women's Day on March 8, 2011: 377 live events in 152 countries. The WIN is now presenting 1,000 Global Women's Summits worldwide from 2011 - 2021. The WIN Motto: "We Are Women Helping Women Live Our Best Lives."

Dr. Paula Fellingham has given presentations to many delegates at the United Nations, for the World Movement of

Mothers in Paris, at the International Conference of the Worldwide Organization for Women, and numerous other conferences across the world. Paula participated in the World Congress on Families in Geneva, and at the World Movement of Mothers International Conference at NATO Headquarters.

Former radio personality, Dr. Paula hosted a daily two-hour show called "Solutions For Families" that achieved the station's highest ratings for a talk show. Additionally, Paula hosted a segment on the nationally-syndicated show "Celebrate!"

Magazine contributor, Paula has written articles for People Magazine, International Business Times, Boston Globe, ABC 11, Worth Magazine, Family Living, Executive Excellence.

Founder of Solutions For Families, Inc, Women Celebrating Life, Inc., Families Now, Inc. and Unlimited Living International, Inc. Former member of the National Board of Directors, Worldwide Organization for Women; State Board of American Mothers, Inc. Paula chaired the Committee for the "Call From The Families Of The World" in conjunction with the World Congress on Families Conference, in Switzerland.

Former Vice President of eFamily.com. Former Executive Director of Families Worldwide Inc, an international non-profit organization that offers resources to strengthen families. Presently, Dr. Paula Fellingham works with the non-profit organization, SUM 1. Their mission is to educate women and girls worldwide.

Producer of The Fellingham Family musical group. Paula's eight-member family band performed across America and internationally for twelve summers. During their final season,

The Fellingham Family presented 273 shows.

Paula received her Bachelor of Arts in 1971, and her Doctorate in 2004. Dr. Gilbert Fellingham (University Professor of Statistics) and Paula are the parents of eight children, and the grandparents of twenty-four grandchildren.

Contact:

Paula@WomensInformationNetwork.com
www.WomensInformationNetwork.com
www.PaulaFellingham.com

Patricia Barnett

Patricia Barnett is a highly sought-after success consultant, speaker, life coach and author who has inspired and helped thousands of people around the world start dreaming again – and then achieve those dreams.

Best known for her unmatched passion for serving others, Patricia taps into her ability to serve as a catalyst, propelling others to action. She is a results expert, helping people to move from a point of just hoping to a point of achieving the success they desire.

As a student of self-development and human potential for nearly twenty years, and among an elite group of top producers in the direct sales industry, Patricia uses her knowledge and experience to help others unlock their personal potential to achieve success, as well as applying it to her very own life, demonstrated by her own success story.

With a dramatic win over deadly illness, Patricia Barnett has relied on her faith and unwavering belief to guide her through life's most daunting challenges, and to ultimately achieve enviable success. In the midst of her health battle, Patricia termed herself a "thriver" – not a mere survivor. She has applied this attitude to every aspect of her life.

Today, Patricia is a Beacon of Hope, sharing her message as a one-on-one coach and to large audiences around the world –

providing support for others to achieve their life's goals and to live as "thrivers" no matter the circumstances. Illustrated by her own experiences of finding strength and courage in the midst of tragedy, her enthusiastic message is that anyone can achieve health, happiness, and success if equipped with the right tools.

Patricia is a dedicated and loving wife to her husband, Richard, and together they have raised two incredible children, Ross and Amber.

Contact:

Patricia@FourDames.com
www.PatriciaBarnett.com
www.FourDames.com

Julie Jones Hamilton

For 24 years, Julie has served thousands of women to reclaim inner-power from substance dependency as a former president and board member of the nationally renowned long-term women's treatment facility, in Lexington KY, *the Chrysalis House*, www.chrysalishouse.org.

The founder of *The Empowerment Foundation Group, LLC,* and *Julie Jones Hamilton International Consulting,* Julie consults professionals, groups, churches, and entrepreneurs to create results, realize dreams, and accelerate success by building a blueprint for a business and a life they love living. She believes everyone has the capacity to become a deliberate co-creator of life's experiences. Julie offers programs, seminars, retreats and workshops and is the co-author of Amazon #1 Bestseller, *"Women Living Consciously II," "The Change" Series* and soon to be published *"The Power of Recovery."*

As founding partner of The Four Dames, together they speak and create workshops, global courses, and spa retreats.

Julie is the recipient of "Dream Builder Achievement Award of Excellence" from the Life Mastery Institute and the "Making A Million Look Small Award" from Gay Hendricks, Bob Proctor, Peggy McColl and Mary Morrissey. She also received the Community Philanthropy Award Appreciation Recognition, Outstanding Service to Women and Children and the University of Kentucky Fellowship Society Award.

Julie Jones Hamilton lives in Lexington Kentucky with her beloved husband, Jimmy, two married daughters Claira and Noelle, a college son Gunnar. Collectively they share eight fabulous children, nineteen grandchildren and six great grandchildren.

Contact:

Julie@FourDames.com
www.JulieJonesHamilton.com
www.FourDames.com

Lynn Kitchen

Lynn Kitchen is passionate about helping clients to realize their "greatness", create wealth and a purposeful life. She is an empowerment specialist helping individuals and businesses to reach greater levels of success and transform their dreams into reality.

Lynn's inspirational keynote talks are a catalyst for creating breakthrough thinking and real results. Lynn has developed an original presentation called the "Café of Dreams" which is sought after at events, seminars and corporate meetings, and is producer of the acclaimed "Cutting Edge Master Mentor Series" and TheCafeofDreams.com, an online meeting place for empowering one's dreams.

Lynn is a founding partner of The Four Dames, a collaborative coaching company helping to empower women worldwide, and a partner in Applied Futurist, an advisory company helping entrepreneurs to broadcast their message to the world. Lynn is also executive producer of NinetyO's.com, an online blog for seniors.

Lynn draws from a 34 year career as an investment advisor and financial executive, and continues to be a Director/Owner of Maxwell Noll Investment Advisors, a money management firm in Pasadena, California. Lynn was one of the first women to have owned her own investment broker-dealer in Los Angeles, California.

Additionally, Lynn taught investment courses to adults for fifteen years at the Pacific School of Finance and served her church community as a state-licensed spiritual practitioner in grief support and renewal for over a decade. Currently Lynn is Board Chair of Spirit Awakening Foundation which brings programs of self-esteem and leadership to incarcerated youth and provides after-prison mentoring and job placement.

Lynn holds a Bachelor of Science, Business Marketing, from California State University, Long Beach, and has held many advanced financial certifications including Licensed Financial Principal as well as additional study toward a Certified Financial Analyst (CFA). Lynn lives in Longboat Key, Florida with her husband and enjoys tennis and biking.

Contact:

Lynn@FourDames.com
www.TheCafeofDreams.com
www.FourDames.com

Marilyn Macha

Executive Coach and Corporate Consultant knows the answer! After 20 years of running one of the top financial services firms in the country, yet finding she felt a longing for more from life, Marilyn has discovered and developed a proven formula for helping high-performing women reach an entirely new level of aliveness and success – both personally and professionally.

Marilyn, nationally acclaimed speaker, author, corporate consultant and certified coach is a visionary and pioneer. Over thirty years ago she began a career in the financial services industry, an industry dominated then and now by men.

In 2014 she sold her very successful financial planning practice in Houston, TX to pursue her consulting and coaching career full time. Already seasoned in supporting her clients through the good years and the challenging times she knew her gift was helping people clearly create lives that exemplify the most meaningful life possible for them and one which would reflect their personal values. Marilyn's many years of observation and study in the fields of psychology, philosophy, neuroscience, quantum physics and mathematics all brought her to the understanding that what we think and what our thinking is about, literally, creates how we experience life.

She has been recognized by many financial publications such as Barron's and Forbes as an outstanding leader in the financial planning field. Marilyn served most recently on the

Advisory Board of Directors of The Monarch School, a non-profit school specializing in developing and teaching children with neurological differences. She has served on many other Boards of organizations that are focused on purposes that transform our world in positive ways. She has supported many local organizations promoting child welfare in Houston.

Marilyn Lives in Lees Summit, Missouri with her Husband John. She has a loving son and daughter-in-law and two grandchildren she adores.

Contact:

Marilyn@FourDames.com
www.MarilynMacha.com
www.FourDames.com